Worlds of Childhood

Worlds of Childhood

THE ART AND CRAFT
OF WRITING FOR CHILDREN

MAURICE SENDAK / ROSEMARY WELLS

JILL KREMENTZ / JEAN FRITZ

JACK PRELUTSKY / KATHERINE PATERSON

Edited with an Introduction by

WILLIAM ZINSSER

A MARINER BOOK
HOUGHTON MIFFLIN COMPANY
BOSTON   NEW YORK

FIRST MARINER BOOKS EDITION 1998

For information about permission to reproduce selections from this book, write to Permissions, Houghton Mifflin Company, 215 Park Avenue South, New York, New York 10003.

Library of Congress Cataloging-in-Publication Data

Worlds of childhood : the art and craft of writing for children / Jean Fritz . . . [et al.] ; edited by William Zinsser.
p.   cm. — (The Writer's craft)
Includes bibliographical references.
Contents: Introduction/William Zinsser — Visitors from my boyhood/Maurice Sendak — The well-tempered children's book/ Rosemary Wells — Listening to children/Jill Krementz — The teller and the tale/Jean Fritz — In search of the addle-pated paddlepuss/Jack Prelutsky — Heart in hiding/Katherine Paterson.
ISBN 0-395-90151-0 (pbk.)
1. Children's literature — Authorship.   I. Sendak, Maurice.
II. Zinsser, William Knowlton.   III. Series.
PN147.5.W65   1989   89-26815
808.06'8 — dc20   CIP

Grateful acknowledgment is made for permission to quote from: *The Great Gilly Hopkins* by Katherine Paterson. Copyright © 1978 by Katherine Paterson. Reprinted by permission of Harper & Row Publishers, Inc. *Park's Quest* by Katherine Paterson. Copyright © 1988 by Katherine Paterson. Reprinted by permission of the publisher, Lodestar Books, an affiliate of Dutton Children's Books, a division of Penguin Books USA Inc. *Caldecott & Co.* by Maurice Sendak. Copyright © 1988 by Maurice Sendak. Reprinted by permission of Farrar, Straus and Giroux, Inc. Jack Prelutsky's poetry: From *Nightmares:* "The Bogeyman." From *Rolling Harvey Down the Hill:* "Willie Ate a Worm." From *Zoo Doings:* "The Egg," "Don't Ever Seize a Weasel by the Tail," "The Cow," "Bees," "The Snail," and "Boing! Boing! Squeak!" From *The New Kid on the*

Printed in the United States of America

QUM 10 9 8 7 6 5 4

Contents

WILLIAM ZINSSER

Introduction

No KIND of writing lodges itself so deeply in our memory, reverberating there for the rest of our lives, as the books that we met in our childhood, and when we grow up and read them to our own children they are the oldest of old friends. In this volume six modern masters of the form, ranging from the toddler's "board book" to the young adult novel, explain how they go about that difficult work.

The book originated in 1989 as a series of talks held at the New York Public Library and conceived by the Book-of-the-Month Club. As director of that annual project I had edited four earlier series into print — on biography, memoir, religious writing, and the political novel — and with *Worlds of Childhood* I used the same method, working from tape-recorded transcripts of the talks. The six speakers had been asked to stay close to their craft of writing and illustrating — to be personal and anecdotal — and as they told their stories it was easy to understand how all of them had become best-selling authors, filling a specific need for young readers.

But the decade since those talks were given has eroded much of the security of childhood. Children's literature is no longer a safe haven from the sordid facts of life. Today those realities come crashing into the home with every newspaper article and newscast and talk show describing addiction, rape, abuse, crime, domestic violence, and sex in high and low places. I wondered how the classic children's writers had survived the unraveling times. Were the six authors represented in *Worlds of Childhood* still pertinent, their books still helpful to the young?

I put my question to Julie Cummins, coordinator of children's services for the New York Public Library. She confirmed my impression that the world of children's literature has darkened considerably. "There's almost no subject now that's taboo," she said. "We're seeing subjects that wouldn't have been touched ten or fifteen years ago. Divorce used to be the most controversial topic; now it's gay parents and early sexual experimentation. We're also seeing more violence and mental distress." She cited two breakthrough bestsellers in the young adult field in 1997: Han Nolan's *Dancing on the Edge*, about a young girl's upbringing in an occult household and her descent into madness, and Brock Cole's *The Facts Speak for Themselves*, the story of a teenage girl contending with a rape and its aftermath.

Far from being dismissed as freakish, both books were honored. Nolan won the National Book Award in the "young people" category and Cole's book was a nominee. "What redeems those books," Cummins told me, "is that they describe highly emotional events in unemotional language. They're not preachy or overwrought. The young reader is accorded respect by the author. The young person has rights."

The word "respect" gave me my answer. As I thought back over the values expressed by all six writers in *Worlds of Childhood*, I was reminded that what gave them their stature in the first place and their continuing position of trust was their respect for the girls and boys they were writing for.

"Those six authors are still at the top of their form and still current," Cummins said. "Maurice Sendak is the single most important children's book creator today. In fact, the history of picture books in

5]

America over the past fifty years is dominated by the two S's — Seuss and Sendak. Rosemary Wells continues to capture the important moments of early childhood, using animals to act out childhood experiences. Jill Krementz set a standard in photographic nonfiction that nobody has surpassed. Her books about children's occupations, like *A Very Young Dancer*, and about their major traumas, like *How It Feels When a Parent Dies*, filled a huge gap in giving children information they need. Jean Fritz was the first children's writer to turn historical figures into lively people. Before her, biographies for young people were stuffy — the characters didn't have any reality. Jack Prelutsky has made poetry enjoyable for children, writing on topics they find fascinating, from dinosaurs to yucky foods. Katherine Paterson's books have won two Newbery awards and two National Book Awards, and that's no accident. She creates dimensional children who speak to the heart."

There's nothing "cute or Disneyfied" about these writers, Cummins pointed out. What propels their work is not the message but the narrative. She cited two recent picture books — one good, one bad — about gay parents. "The good one has a message, but the message is part of the story; it's done with respect for the child. The other book is dreadfully illustrated and very didactic — the message drives the story."

[6

Messages are the death of an honest literary transaction with children. The two questions that Katherine Paterson gets asked most often are: "What message are you trying to teach children through your books?" and "What moral values are you trying to impart to young readers?" She says, "I try not to get testy. What I think I'm doing when I write a book for the young is to connect with the part of the child that's hidden. I'm trying to write a story."

"First do no harm," says the doctor's Hippocratic oath. If writers of children's books had to take an oath it might begin, "First tell the truth." One insistent theme in *Worlds of Childhood* is that children are wiser than adults think they are. They know when they are being lied to, condescended to, equivocated with; they know a fudged fact when they see it or hear it.

"People said *Dear Mili* should be kept from children," Maurice Sendak says, "because it has a fearful ending — because Mili dies. But anyone who thinks that children don't worry, don't ponder, don't obsess about dying, who thinks Grimm's tale is going to put that thought in their mind, seems to me incredibly naive. Children are extremely tough. They know exactly what's going to frighten their parents, and they don't ask questions that will upset them. You don't want to give your parents ulcers with questions they can't deal with. So you find out in the back yard. Isn't it kinder to give children the bitter pill in a work of art?"

Sendak operates on the assumption that young people know what he is up to and will relate to his own unresolved fears. In a career of ostensibly writing books for children, he has really been writing books for himself, trying to make sense of his childhood and of the strangely disturbing figures who populated it, like the Dionne quintuplets. *Outside Over There* was an attempt to work through an event that had shadowed his life since the age of three — the macabre death of the kidnapped Lindbergh baby. His method is to cloak these specters from the past in a new identity and thereby put them to rest. When the monsters of *Where the Wild Things Are* materialized on Sendak's drawing board he had no trouble recognizing them as Jewish relatives — the uncles and aunts who ruined every Sunday dinner by pinching and poking him and his brother and his sister and saying "those tedious, boring things that grown-ups say."

Such early traumas and needs turned out to be the primary source of material for most of these authors. The child they are writing for is the child they once were. Jean Fritz, born of missionary parents in

China and reared there until she was thirteen, always hearing about "home," felt like a girl without a country, and it was to look for her roots that she started writing biographies of America's founders. For her, writing is "a spiraling process, circling away from oneself, circling back with messages from afar, and all the time circling around one's own autobiography."

Jack Prelutsky admits that animals appear in his poems improbably often for someone who grew up in the Bronx. But the fact is that he lived near the Bronx Zoo and spent much of his boyhood there; that's the kid he is still writing animal poems for. Even so bizarre a creature as his "addle-pated paddlepuss," which plays Ping-Pong with its face, didn't come from nowhere. Nothing in children's literature does. Prelutsky's subconscious mind summoned back a Ping-Pong-playing cat that he saw as a boy on the TV show *You Asked for It*.

Jill Krementz recalls that as a girl she had no access to the kind of books she now writes; they didn't exist. Her reading consisted of fiction and fantasy — books like the Nancy Drew series and *The Secret Garden* that were as guileless as the era she grew up in. That unhelpful diet made her a lifelong rebel. "I've been determined that children reading books today won't be as deprived of reality as I was," she says. "I would rather see children saddened by honesty than angered by omissions or lies." In her book *How It Feels When a Parent Dies* a young boy who lost his mother says he asked himself whether, if it could happen again, it would be better if his father died. "Another child reading that passage," Krementz says, "might have had the same thought and yet, discussing it with his mother or father, might say, 'Boy, can you believe that kid said such an awful thing?' And you hope it's the wise and perceptive parent who says, 'Of course I can. I'd be surprised if you didn't think that yourself sometimes; it would be only natural.'" The child is given permission to think what he or she thought was unthinkable.

"Kids will believe almost anything you tell them, provided you make it truthful," says Rosemary Wells, adding a few Hippocratic rules of her own. A picture book is in trouble, she says, if it's bland or if its tone is false and hysterical, or if it's cute, or if it uses television characters, or if it's written by anybody with a degree in child psychology. "A good picture book must ring with emotional content, so that children care about what's going on."

But what finally underlies all good children's books is language. However vividly we recall the pictures in the books of our childhood, what makes them work is a story that somebody wrote. *Goodnight, Moon,* by Margaret Wise Brown, is a text about saying goodnight to the world. *Millions of Cats,* by Wanda Gág, a book teeming with drawings of cats, takes its life from words — from the idea of millions of cats. Dorothy Kunhardt's *Pat the Bunny* had to be written before there was a bunny to pat.

"With me, everything begins with writing," Maurice Sendak says. "No pictures at all. You don't want to be seduced by pictures because then you begin to write for pictures. Images come in language, language, language: in phrases, in verbal constructs, in poetry, whatever. I've never spent less than two years on the text of one of my picture books, even though each of them is approximately 380 words long. Only when the text is finished do I begin the pictures."

Being so fundamental, language must be fiercely protected from the guardians of what children can or can't understand. Jean Fritz, doing research on Paul Revere, found that one of the British soldiers who stopped him on his midnight ride said, "Sir, may I crave your name?" Fritz was charmed by that eighteenth-century usage and felt that children who didn't know the word would be smart enough to figure it out. But no such assumption was made by the "hedgehogs," as she calls the "prickly, small-minded" creatures who stand watch over the world of textbooks. Appraising her biography for use in schools, they ruled that "crave" was confusing. Hedgehogs, she warns, are the enemy in the temple, their red pencils perpetually poised.

There's nothing accidental about the hold wielded over successive generations of young readers by Edward Lear, L. Frank Baum, Hugh Lofting, Beatrix Potter, A. A. Milne, E. B. White, and other writers who loved language for its own sake and knew that children love it no less. Children enjoy being surprised by an unusual word. Even if they don't know what it means, they appreciate the writer's effort to entertain them with language and not to patronize them.

One of my favorite nonpatronizers is Hugh Lofting. In his Doctor Dolittle books he never hesitates to use a word that amuses him, as in the Chief Chimpanzee's reaction to hearing that in England the organ grinders' monkeys have to ask for money: "Who would wish to live in such a land? My gracious, how paltry!" Beatrix Potter was also a master of the precise and unexpected word. Pick almost any sentence from *Peter Rabbit*: "His sobs were overheard by some friendly sparrows, who flew to him in great excitement, and implored him to exert himself." The language is as bracing as the danger in Mr. McGregor's garden.

Jack Prelutsky's gift to children is pure enjoyment of words for their sound. The nonsense poems of Edward Lear are obviously the legacy he has claimed as his own. His meters are tidy, and near the end of his poems a small surprise often lies in wait:

> *Clankity clankity clankity clank!*
> *Ankylosaurus was built like a tank,*
> *Its hide was a fortress as sturdy as steel,*
> *It tended to be an inedible meal.*

That quatrain from *Tyrannosaurus Was a Beast,* a collection of dinosaur poems, is typical of the antic language — and the humor — with which Prelutsky has befriended preschoolers and their parents in more than thirty books. Rhythm and cadence are at the heart of his writing. "The sound of a word," he says, "is at least as important as the meaning."

Much wailing is heard today over the fact that "nobody can write well anymore." One reason is that parents don't read aloud to their children as much as they once did. The voice heard at bedtime is more often the voice of television, gratefully used as a babysitter by mothers and fathers exhausted by their jobs. But to write well it is necessary to grow up hearing how other people have written well: to get into one's metabolism the grandeur, the playfulness, and the narrative strength of the English language. No age is too early to start. Infants are ready for the lilt of words.

Again and again the writers in this book come back to language. Katherine Paterson recalls that she was primarily influenced by the poetry of Gerard Manley Hopkins, learning "how language works on the mind and the heart and the ear." She was also influenced by the Bible. "I don't think morality is the basic theme of the Bible," she says. "It's closer to what physicists call beauty. The first question that physicists ask of a new theory is: 'Is it beautiful?' For experience has taught them that truth is invariably beautiful." Beauty is defined by physicists as having simplicity, harmony, and brilliance. Those are also the properties that Paterson feels are crucial to good writing, brilliance being "the light that a book sheds not only on itself but beyond itself to other stories and other lives." Thus what we ultimately want of a children's book is nothing less than beauty — the sum of what is best in nature and in ourselves.

MAURICE SENDAK

Visitors from My Boyhood

Today somebody reminded me that this year is the fiftieth anniversary of *The Wizard of Oz*. I was glad to hear that, not only because it's one of my all-time favorite movies, but because I'm writing a film script and I'm just at the moment when, dramatically, something happens that's similar to what occurs in the movies. I've borrowed from everybody during my career, so I shouldn't have been surprised to find myself stealing from a movie. But in this case I was taking the very scene that charged me and moved me when I first saw *The Wizard of Oz*. It's a scene that stole into my life in 1939 and has been flooding my work continually ever since.

I was eleven when I saw the movie, and I remember

it vividly because of how intensely it frightened me. Of course it was a sensational fear — I would have killed anyone who tried to take me out of the movie house. The moment I'm talking about is the one when Dorothy is trapped by the Wicked Witch of the West, and the witch takes an hourglass and turns it over and says something horrible like, "When the sand runs out, you're dead, honey." Judy Garland is left alone in the room, and one of her best moments ever was her way of saying, "I'm frightened," and then, as though that realization has just actually dawned on her, says it a second time: "I'm frightened." I still remember how her hand went to her head — the way she had of fluttering her hand, her desperation was so convincing. There was no way out of that room, nothing she could do. And suddenly, in the witch's crystal ball, she sees her Auntie Em, back in Kansas, standing in the yard and calling to her. And she rushes to the crystal ball and stands over it and screams, "Auntie Em! Here I am!"

Well, that just killed me, because they couldn't get together. I was too young to know that it was a metaphor. I only knew that it was the most frustrating moment in history: that Auntie Em couldn't save Dorothy, even though they were connected through the crystal ball. At the end of the movie there's another moment that's almost as vivid to me. Dorothy is back in Kansas, and she's safe, and she's lying in bed, and her family is hovering over her and they're so happy to see her, and she keeps saying, "Gee, I saw this," and she keeps telling them about Oz, and they don't want to hear it. They had been worried about her, and she's describing a death vision she's had. They don't want to know Dorothy was that close to death. But *we* know, because Frank Morgan says to her uncle, "Hey, you nearly lost Dorothy, didn't you?" Which means, of course, that she nearly died. And they won't listen to her.

The last words in *The Wizard of Oz* are Dorothy's words: "There's no place like home." That ending has been criticized as being too sentimental, but I thought it was a brilliant, ironic ending. Because what Dorothy is saying is, "However faulty these people are, this is all I've got." That profoundly affected me, and I think that in every book I've done — or at least in the books that matter most to me — there is that moment when the child is with the mother and they are *that* close together but they're a million miles apart. That's a confrontation that occurs every day in every child's life and every parent's life. The mother loves the kid, the kid loves the mother, but it has to happen that a collision occurs and they don't say the things they want to say, and they don't touch each other at the right moment, and something gets lost. I'm sure that's what it meant to me when I saw the movie fifty years ago, and right now, in 1989, I have this boy in my script going through an experience that's almost precisely the same.

The other day a woman told me she had bought one of my monsters — a doll from *Where the Wild Things Are* — and brought it home and has it sitting in a Louis XV chair. "Children come into the room," she told me, "and they're all frightened by him." I said, "Maybe they're frightened because he's sitting in a Louis XV chair." She said no, it was the monster that frightened them, and she wanted to know how I created the "wild things" in that book.

Originally I didn't want them to be wild "things"; I wanted them to be wild horses. In fact, the original title was *Where the Wild Horses Are*. The dilemma arose when it became obvious that I couldn't draw horses. So I had to think of something I *could* draw. Because the truth about the creative process is that it's a hard-line, nitty-gritty business of what you can and cannot do — what your limitations are as an artist. I tried to use monsters from the antique world — griffins and other such creatures. But they weren't satisfactory because they didn't come out of me; they were borrowed monsters.

Then, very gradually, these other creatures began to appear on my drawing paper, and I knew right away that they were my relatives. They were my uncles and aunts. It wasn't that they were monstrous people; it was simply that I didn't care for them when I was a child because they were rude, and because they ruined every Sunday, and because they ate all our food. They pinched us and poked us and said those tedious, boring things that grown-ups say, and my sister and my brother and I sat there in total dismay and rage. The only fun we had was later, giggling over their grotesque faces — the huge noses, the spiraling hair pouring out of the wrong places. So I know who those "wild things" are. They are Jewish relatives.

People think I have some magic link to my childhood. If there is such a link, it's a process that bypasses my conscious mind, because I have very little real recollection. I couldn't stop and tell you why I'm writing and drawing certain episodes; they're coming from some inner source that *does* recollect.

Music is another powerful source for me. Of all the arts, it's the one I love the most and feel closest to. It's a private force that feeds me while I'm drawing pictures; it fuels my energy and it always has. I'd give anything to have been gifted musically. One reason I design operas is that it gets me close to those composers I love; I can design their sets and design their costumes. What I can't do, obviously, is convey music in my work, and this somehow bothers some readers. Several of them have asked me, for instance, why I don't show Mozart in *Dear Mili* playing an instrument. What they don't know, because it's known only to me, is that Mozart is conducting a choir of children from the French village of Izieu whom the Nazi Klaus Barbie murdered just before the end of World War II. I became absorbed with the fate of those children during Barbie's trial a couple of years ago, and when I illustrated *Dear Mili* I took some of them and put them in paradise with Mozart, who is my favorite creature in the whole world. And Mili is there, and her guardian angel is there, and all these good guys are there. So music is in the book emblematically through the figure of Wolfgang Amadeus Mozart.

People have said that *Dear Mili* should be kept from children because it has a fearful ending — because Mili dies. I think it's a book eminently for children. Anyone who thinks that children don't worry, don't ponder, don't obsess about dying, who thinks that Grimm's tale is going to put that thought in their mind, seems to me incredibly naïve. I'll tell you the reaction of the first little girl who saw *Dear Mili*. She did cry, and her mother said, "Are you unhappy because Mili died?" and she said, "No, no." She knew that from the beginning — she knew there was no other way for the book to end. What she *was* crying about was, why did the rose have to die? Why didn't they put it in water before they went to bed? It's just the pragmatic business of being a child: Does everybody have to die? Couldn't the rose have survived?

Children are extremely tough — they know exactly what's going to frighten their parents, and they don't ask questions that will upset mommy and daddy. They see the signs on their parents' faces: "Uh-oh, distress time coming." I remember from my own childhood that I would never tell my parents anything that disturbed me because it would have upset them. And since you love and honor your parents, you don't want to give them ulcers with questions they can't deal with. So you find out in the back yard, or from the landlady's daughter. But you do find out. Even before television, you found out. Isn't it kinder to give children the bitter pill in a work of art?

Higglety Pigglety Pop! is also a book about death,

the death of my terrier, Jennie. Nobody seemed to understand that. When the book came out it got very erudite reviews — so erudite that I didn't understand some of them. None of them, however, mentioned the simple fact that the dog died. But my niece, who was six at the time and who spent a good deal of her childhood in my house, refused to talk to me, because Jennie was my dog, and she adored Jennie, and she couldn't believe that while Jennie was living I would write a book about her death. She knew instantly that the book was about that dog dying. It's the way children dive into symbology or metaphor — they just go; they get it. They may not like what they get, but they know how to go right to the heart of the matter.

So why *did* I write the book? Jennie was getting on, and I was worried about her dying. I feel that art is a kind of magic; if you make magic you'll keep somebody alive. So the book was to keep Jennie alive. Also, she had appeared in almost every book of mine since I got her in 1953. She had made little cameo appearances — sometimes very inappropriately — and it seemed only fair that in her dotage and in her great loyalty to me she should have her own book. Beyond that, *Higglety Pigglety Pop!* was my contemplation of Jennie's death — of what was going to happen to her — and I tried to think, "What could I provide for her that would make her happiest?"

[24

Well, the thing she loved most was eating. She loved eating far more than she loved me, which was a bitter pill — the kind of thing we all find out eventually about our relationships and then keep to ourselves. In this case I knew that Jennie would go to somebody else's house if the food was better. We know that sort of thing about our wives and our husbands and our children; we also know it about our dogs, and I take my dogs very seriously. Therefore, to do justice to Jennie, I had to acknowledge that food was uppermost. As the book begins, when she leaves my house and says, "There must be more to life than having everything," she means food. Better fare. Just a nicer place to hang out.

So the book was a portrait of Jennie — of her character — and of what I wished for her. My wish was that she would be an actress and that she would go on stage somewhere off in the cosmos and perform her little show throughout eternity, and twice on Saturdays, and that the mop she swallows would be made of salami, her favorite food, and that she could eat it every day. What more could I wish for her?

That was the subsoil of *Higglety Pigglety Pop!* At that time I was very interested in English book illustration, particularly in a group of men who made exquisite engravings. That period of book illustration came to be called the Sixties, meaning the 1860s, which was the historical moment when they all seemed to flower at the same place. What characterized their work was superb technique and a highly romantic kind of interpretation. The movement lasted only ten years, and I gathered it all up in one book and copied their style. It's the book of mine that most pointedly emulates a particular technique and period.

My reason for choosing that style was that I wanted it to play against the writing. I wanted the writing to be as terse and as tough as Jennie was, almost acidic — to contain nothing sentimental or romantic. But because *I* brought so much sentiment to the story I wanted the pictures to be as romantic as the text was terse. And they are. The illustrations are doing what the text is not doing; it's a matter of reading between the lines. All the sentiment is in the crosshatching.

The Mother Goose rhyme enacted in Jennie's show is so simple-minded that anyone might wonder why I chose it. This is how it goes:

Higglety pigglety pop!
The dog has eaten the mop.
The cat's in a hurry,

> *The pig's in a flurry,*
> *Higglety pigglety pop!*

I went to Mother Goose because I'm very fond of those rhymes; I keep going back to them as a source. But I chose this one for only one reason: there was a mop to be eaten. I went through all the verses looking for something that somebody ate, and this was the only one. So Jennie was stuck with having to perform that ridiculous verse.

As it turned out, by a delightful coincidence, that verse was written in 1846 by an American deacon named Samuel Griswold Goodrich, who lived in Ridgefield, Connecticut, which is where I now live. Goodrich was violently opposed to fairy tales and nursery rhymes. He denounced them so strongly that by the early years of the nineteenth century he had almost single-handedly gotten them banished from the nurseries of England and America. One day he said from his pulpit, "These nursery rhymes are so disgraceful and stupid that any jackass" — I guess he meant someone like himself — "could make one up right here," and he made up "Higglety Pigglety Pop!" on the spot. Somebody in the church wrote it down, and lo and behold, Goodrich's worst fears have come true. Not only has he become a Mother

Goose rhymer himself; a century later somebody comes to live in his own village and despoils him even further by writing a book with that title. I think it's terrific justice.

With me, everything begins with writing. No pictures at all — you just shut the Polaroid off; you don't want to be seduced by pictures because then you begin to write for pictures. Images come in language, language, language: in phrases, in verbal constructs, in poetry, whatever. I've never spent less than two years on the text of one of my picture books, even though each of them is approximately 380 words long. Only when the text is finished — when my editor thinks it's finished — do I begin the pictures. *Then* I put the film in my head.

I've illustrated many books that I didn't write — books by such extraordinary writers as Randall Jarrell; Ruth Krauss, who wrote *A Hole Is to Dig;* Else Holmelund Minarik, who wrote the Little Bear books; and Isaac Bashevis Singer. I was lucky to collaborate with these writers. I learned my trade by working with them.

It was extraordinary to work with Singer on *Zlateh the Goat.* It was his first collection of stories for children, and I think it's one of his finest books. Of course my parents had read Singer, because his work ran in the *Jewish Daily Forward* in the original Yiddish. This was lovely for me, because it was a project that my parents could be involved in, and they were enormously proud that I was doing it. One of the pleasures of working with Singer was hearing Yiddish spoken when he first read me his stories. Though I had grown up with Yiddish, I now realized that my parents' Yiddish was rough-and-tumble, whereas his was cultivated and very beautiful.

I was already making children's books when I was a little boy; it was all I could do. It alarmed my father, because he had three children, and two of them, my brother and I, only wrote stories and drew pictures. My sister was the regular one — good looking, passing grades — and then there were these two dud sons who stayed upstairs and had green complexions. My brother was the writer, and from a very early age I would do drawings to accompany his stories. Then he would read them aloud to the family and I'd hold up the pictures, which were done on shirt cardboards. That's all we had to draw on, so they were always shirt-cardboard-size illustrations.

The first "real" book I illustrated, when I was fourteen, was Oscar Wilde's *The Happy Prince* — my own private edition, copyright and everything. Then I did Bret Harte's *The Luck of Roaring Camp*, which was one of my favorite stories, and then Charpentier's opera *Louise*. I never studied or did my homework; I had terrible grades in school. All I wanted to do was sit home and draw, and that's all I've done ever since. The only thing that has changed is that my hair has turned gray.

The major event of my childhood was the kidnapping of the Lindbergh baby in 1932. That nightmare was probably the origin of my conviction that children can't be shielded from frightening truths. Back in the thirties we only had the radio and newspapers to tell us what was going on in the world. Still, though I was only three, I remember intensely the details of the Lindbergh case. The whole world was held in suspense. Would the baby be returned alive? How could such a thing happen to this fabulous family? Lindbergh was our Prince Charles, and his wife was our Princess Di, and this was our royal prince. When the news came that the baby was dead, it was just not to be believed. I rejected the information because I so badly wanted him to come home alive.

I particularly remember a newspaper that had the front-page headline LINDBERGH BABY FOUND DEAD and a photograph of a scene in the woods with a black arrow pointing to something awful. I've since learned that Colonel Lindbergh threatened to sue if the *New York Daily News* didn't have the morning edition pulled off the newsstands, so I guess not many people saw the picture. But *I* saw the picture. Many years later, when I was in therapy, my psychiatrist assumed that this was part of my problem — that I had this image in my head of something that had never existed.

Well, about five years ago I met a man named Anthony Scaduto who had written a book that exonerated Bruno Richard Hauptmann, the German carpenter who was sentenced to death for the kidnapping and murder. Scaduto came to give a talk at my local library, and I kept raising my hand and asking questions. When it was over he said, "I think we should go out and have a cup of coffee." We did, and we got to be very friendly, and later he shared some of the information he had in his files.

Eventually the question of the newspaper photograph came up, and I felt that he was the person who could resolve it for me. "All my life I've had this memory of a hideous image of the corpse," I said. "I saw it as a small child, but my parents deny it, like Auntie Em, and my therapist thinks I'm crazy, and so do a lot of other people."

"No, you saw it," Scaduto said, and he told me the story of that early edition of the *News*. "What did the picture look like?" he wanted to know. I described it and then drew it for him. The next time we met he showed me the photograph. My sketch duplicated the scene almost exactly.

The Lindbergh case was one of the inspirations for my book *Outside Over There*. Among other things, that book is about the fear children have of being separated from mommy and daddy — the fear of being lost. The safest child in the world has that anxiety. During the Second World War, I kept badgering my father by asking, "Will you die, too?" Finally, just to shut me up, he said he wouldn't. It's a question every child worries about.

So, in *Outside Over There*, I decided that I was going to change history. Ida would bring the Lindbergh baby back alive. It didn't happen in real life, but it happens in my book. I've been criticized for giving the book a happy ending — the father's letter. But it's not a "happy ending"; it's a very ironic ending. It's typical of a macho papa to write and say, "Honey, you take care of everything. Do it for me. I love you a lot. Thanks." In this case a nine-year-old girl is stuck with the problem. *Outside Over There* wasn't intended to be a cheerful, upbeat book. It was intended to be a book about a serious question that has always been part of my life.

I also put various other elements of the thirties into *Outside Over There*. For instance, it was the decade of babies. There was Fanny Brice as Baby Snooks, and there was Eddie Cantor, who used any excuse to get dressed up like a baby. If you look at movies of the period, everyone's in a high chair with a rattle or wearing a baby bonnet. I'd like some sociologist to figure out why. Then, in the midst of all that, Canada was saved from bankruptcy by the miracle of the Dionne quintuplets. They were so valuable, so rare — five identical creatures from one egg — and it happened under such primitive, rural conditions. The whole world stopped for those five babies. You lived from day to day to see whether they had survived. If one of them had colic, you held your breath. We weren't thinking about Hitler invading Austria or any of the other terrible events that were taking place in the world. We focused our attention on what was bearable and fantastic, and that was the Dionnes. On top of everything, they were exquisitely beautiful. They were so beautiful that the government took them away from their parents and made them into an industry — until they grew up and were ordinary looking, and then they were sent back to their parents.

While I was working on *Outside Over There* my sister came to visit. I showed her the pictures and she immediately recognized herself as Ida. She had been that demonic, though she's a nice, mostly civilized lady now. And when she saw the five goblin babies she automatically said, "Yvonne, Marie, Cecile, Emilie and Annette." After all, that was our childhood. The only thing we ever really fought over was the set of "quint" spoons. After our parents died there was a struggle over who would get Émilie and who would get Yvonne. That was as Balzacian as we ever got.

My sister was also responsible for bringing into our house the book that was my favorite reading as a boy — after *Mickey Mouse in Pygmyland* — though I couldn't read a word of it. It was *Kristin Lavransdatter* by Sigrid Undset. My sister is nine years older than I am, and she belonged to the Book-of-the-Month Club. I was very jealous of the packages that came in the mail for her. I was jealous that these were books that belonged to her, books that she could put on her side of the shelf and that were forbidden to my brother and me.

[34

I don't know why I made such a big scene over *Kristin Lavransdatter*. Maybe because it was the fattest book I ever saw. Certainly it was very beautiful. It was bound in pale green cloth, and on the spine it had KRISTIN LAVRANSDATTER in gold with two black stripes; I could paint it for you right now. Anyway, I carried on so that my parents forced my sister to let me have it. What I did with it, since I was too young to read, was to turn the pages. When I felt that an appropriate amount of time had passed — the time an adult would take — I'd turn to the next page. My sister didn't get that book back for a long time, and when she finally did it had been abused — licked and sniffed and mauled — because it was so gorgeous. I couldn't believe that a book could be such a beautiful, fat item. Years later I sat down and really read it, and I loved it. But the second reading wasn't as good as the first.

I didn't read any children's books when I was a child, only comic books and cartoon books that were based on Hollywood characters like Mickey Mouse, Betty Boop and Felix the Cat. I didn't get to know children's literature until I was in my twenties and earning my living as an illustrator. I was impressed by the wide scope of what I read and saw, but I was most inspired by what I knew best: my Brooklyn childhood. *The Sign on Rosie's Door*, for in-

35]

stance, is entirely autobiographical. There was a real Rosie, and she did live across the street from us. During the war I was very lonely because my brother, who was my best friend, had gone into the army. So I would just sit by the window all day and sketch what I saw, and one of the things I saw was Rosie.

She was extremely entertaining — and tough — and she made her friends by being an actress. She was surrounded by kids who were not her equal in imagination and intelligence, but she was doomed, like the rest of them, to incarceration on one Brooklyn block. You couldn't cross the street, you couldn't go anywhere, so you had to make do with what you had. Rosie was the classic example of making do with what you've got. What she did was to turn everybody on her side of the street into an audience for herself.

One day she was sitting on the stoop with her friends, and suddenly — I could hear everything from my window — she said, "Did I tell you who died?" A great first line. She said, "My grandmother died." I was taken aback, because I knew her grandmother. I saw her every morning beating the pillows. It was a loud, vociferous Sicilian family, and the grandmother was a huge woman who was always beating pillows. One of the kids said, "What happened?"

[36

Rosie went into the pillow act. She said, "My grand-mother was up there early in the morning. Nobody else was around, and she started beating on a pillow and she lost her breath and started to choke and fell back into the room. I was the first one who found her, because she weighs a ton and her bedroom is on top of mine, and I heard this *clonk*. I ran upstairs and she was dead and I had to call the hospital." It was totally convincing.

Just then, as luck would have it, Rosie's grand-mother came up the street. She had two big shopping bags. She was a very curt woman — she didn't speak any English — and when she got to the stoop where the kids were sitting she made this rough gesture, like "Get the hell out of my way," and they parted like the Red Sea and she went up into the house. The kids came back and said, "Hey, Rosie! Tell us how your grandmother died!" She was a finished artist already.

ROSEMARY WELLS

The Well-Tempered Children's Book

This is not an idly chosen title, nor is it meant to be catchy. Bach's melodies — to me the most beautiful melodies in music — emerge from a tightly constructed foundation. Some people find them cold because of their perfection. But all fine works of music, dance, painting and literature are born not from vague inspiration but — as I see it in my mind's eye — from a design as clean and spare as a house frame of New Hampshire birch. Children's picture books are a short literary form like the sonnet. The soundness of their structure is therefore crucial — more important than in longer and more leisurely forms of writing.

I want to begin with Max and Ruby. I can pinpoint

exactly when Max and Ruby surfaced. Our daughter Victoria was five years old and still reverberating from the birth of Marguerite, who was by then and is still mysteriously called Beezoo. That name, Beezoo, just flew through the air one day and stuck to her like a burr. Anyway, nine months old and five years old — an age difference custom-designed to give the older child such an upper hand that the younger one doesn't have much of a chance. Fortunately, Beezoo was built like a small jet engine and had nerves of steel.

Victoria was never openly jealous because, officially being the absolute boss, there's nothing to be jealous of. She took in hand Beezoo's training. Talking, dressing, eating and going on stroller rides were Victoria's province whenever we let her, and the sessions were conducted much as they would be at Parris Island. Beezoo was hauled like a sack of flour and propped up in front of objects, her older sister repeating their names imperiously. But Beezoo would never say "table" or "chair" or "dog." She only said "da-da" and, unaccountably, "Rockefeller." She wouldn't put any clothes *on;* she would only take them off. She had to be double-buckled into a stroller, with a harness put on backwards and safety-pinned, because she was a natural Houdini. As for training Beezoo to eat politely, Victoria tried and lost that one, too.

I had written a picture book that summer. I put every ounce of love, wit and lyricism in my jittery soul into that book. It was a real loser. I had wanted to write about an old woman who digs in her heels and hangs on to her house in the face of avaricious developers who want to tear it down. It wasn't that this was a poor idea; it's just that writing *about* anything is a mistake. The only books that work are those which fly through the air — the ones you *let* happen, not *make* happen. Phyllis Fogelman, who has been my editor for eighteen years, turned it down in the nicest way she knows, which is to say she loves it but it has five terminal flaws and could I put it in a drawer for a while?

The next day I was very depressed. Rejection is borne well by strong people with healthy egos, and I don't have any of that. On my drawing table were a few pieces of illustration board left over from my previous book. Suddenly a bunny appeared on one of them. I finished his face and clothed him. I was listening to Handel and not thinking about this silly rabbit at all. Then all of what was happening downstairs — Victoria as Emily Post, the dining etiquette, the vocabulary lessons — came floating upstairs like a sonata and appeared on sixteen square-cut four-by-four boards as *Max's First Word*.

In the morning I took this sixteen-page oddity to Phyllis. (Let me say one thing about working regularly with the same editor and publisher. One reason it suits me is that when I do write something that Phyllis rejects, which mercifully almost never happens anymore, I don't get angry and take it to another editor. I write something better.) On this occasion I couldn't yet understand what had happened. I had created what was clearly a picture book, but it was only sixteen pages long and wasn't for the usual nursery school and kindergarten crew. Picture books were thirty-two pages long, some even forty. For two months I had poured my heart and soul into the manuscript about the old lady and gotten nowhere. In six hours Victoria had become Ruby and Beezoo had become Max — at a time when I was trying my best to "work" and to ignore them.

Usually Phyllis is very talkative. This time she just laughed and then stared at the book. "It's a complete innovation," she said at last. "All books for very young toddlers have one word per page and deadly dull pictures of objects. Even an eighteen-month-old can be bored by a boring book. But this is funny! And it's a real story. Go home and write three more and we'll do something that nobody has done in publishing before." What Phyllis had seen in an instant was

[44

that the essence of a good picture book can be distilled, halved in length and printed on sturdy material for children who are just learning to talk and to understand but who aren't too young to be read to.

I went home and three other books — *Max's Ride, Max's New Suit* and *Max's Toys* — all rushed onto the little square boards like tiny actors who had been waiting in the wings for their turn on the stage. Thus was born what came to be known in book circles as "board books" — books that could survive a certain amount of infant vandalizing without coming apart and, even more important, could make mothers and fathers and their babies laugh at themselves and each other and the world around them.

After that it was relatively easy, several years later, to follow the first four books with four more, because bathing, bedtime, birthdays and eating-what-you-hate hadn't been covered. More would have been redundant. Today Max and Ruby have graduated to two twenty-four-page picture books, simply because all the very young stories were used up.

I don't mean to imply that you need to have children around in order to write children's books. Beatrix Potter didn't have any children. Neither did Margaret

Wise Brown, or Maurice Sendak, or many other giants of children's literature. If William Steig ever had children, they must be older than I am. Books come from absolutely everywhere. For me, they become children's books simply because that's the voice I have. You can be a superb writer and not have a voice for poetry, or for nonfiction or journalism. Children's books are a field of writing like any other, but they're not easier to do because they are for children, in the same way that making lunch for children might be easier to do.

Writing for very young children is the most difficult discipline I know. Kids will believe almost anything you tell them — provided you make it truthful. That may sound bland, but there's a catch. There really aren't many people who can do this arcane and specialized kind of writing, yet thousands of people aspire to it. This is because they love and have or are around children all day and love the literature written for them. But that's not enough. Being around adults and loving novels, for instance, doesn't make a writer out of everyone who has a flair for putting words on paper. There is a misperception that children's books are a sort of muzzy and not-quite-serious art form. They are as hard to write and edit, however, as good poetry. Like poetry, they must not have a single un-

[46

needed syllable in any line. A poem, which is a kind of chain, is as strong as its weakest rhyme or meter, whereas in a long prose work a bit of unevenness can be hidden. One false note ruins a poem. The same is true of picture book stories.

Writing well for children must be learned. There are rules. I consider myself lucky to have come into this field in the late sixties, which was the golden age of children's writing and illustration. Probably the most influential editor in the field was the late Ursula Nordstrom of Harper & Row. The books she published began a revolution in children's literature. Equally important, the editors she trained have inspired a new generation of writers and illustrators. I never met Ursula Nordstrom, but I feel that I know her well because her ideas have trickled down to me through her books and through her many disciples.

I mentioned that there are rules for writing picture books. Every time I don't go by these rules I burn the tips of my fingers.

First of all, a good picture book must ring with emotional content, so that children care about what's going on. Otherwise they will fall asleep. William Steig's *Amos and Boris* and *Sylvester and the Magic Pebble* never fail to overwhelm a reader with both worry and love. They can't be put down; they work beautifully every time. What is in them is in all of us: guilt, fear, devotion. As a writer you have little time and few pages to achieve this. The characters in a children's book must reach into the heart of the reader on page one. Emotional content is the main reason a child and a parent will go back to a book again and again.

A story for children must also be short enough to be read without giving the reader a need for sips of water between pages. I can't tell you how many times my kids used to truck out some gorgeous book with stunning pictures that took half an hour to read and how often, not without guilt, I said, "How about *Goodnight, Moon* instead?" When I conduct a workshop there's one book that is the perfect teaching book for brevity: Robert Kraus's *Whose Mouse Are You?*, which was published almost twenty years ago by Macmillan when I happened to be on the staff. José Aruego did the pictures. It has humor, plot, character, pathos and a surprise ending — and it's sixteen lines long.

Not all good picture books are funny, but I think the best ones are. Nothing is as satisfying as making somebody laugh. When somebody has been crying or is overtired or bored to tears by Wednesday afternoon's arithmetic lesson, it's gratifying to make him laugh. To place in the hands of a weary mom or dad

[48

or teacher the means to do it is to give him or her a spiritual gold coin.

All really good picture books are written to be read five hundred times. A picture book is in trouble if it's longer than eight double-spaced typewritten pages. It's also in trouble if it's bland, or if the tone is false and hysterical. It must never be cute or it will insult children. It's in trouble if it uses television characters, or if it's written by anybody with a degree in child psychology. I think the nicest thing a child has told me about my books is that he liked them because they weren't like schoolbook stories, and even if they were about mice or raccoons, they were much more real than the people in those textbooks.

Max and Ruby became books through some osmosis of events taken whole and virtually unchanged by me. *Timothy Goes to School,* however, and *Hazel's Amazing Mother* are different; they are about something deeper. They are about that happens in first and second grade. That's when our classrooms and school playgrounds turn into heated petri dishes for the determination of the school pecking order and the alleviation of huge gobs of personal tension. Timothy and Benjamin — of *Timothy Goes to School* and *Benjamin and Tulip* — are echoes of my grade school years. But more directly, Timothy comes from something that happened in our daughter Victoria's first grade class. In this case, one line was enough for the whole book to materialize.

Victoria was a careful dresser. My mother had bought her an expensive frothy dress for the lower-school Christmas concert. Victoria hated the dress and refused to be seen in it. I said, "O.K., you don't have to wear it, but you do have to conform to the school's dress code, which is no pants or denim or anything casual looking." The next morning she boarded the bus in a lace-trimmed blouse and her favorite plaid kilt, white tights and patent-leather shoes. At noon, as the girls were lining up backstage to sing for the parents a medley of twenty-eight traditional Christmas carols from Japan, another girl, Melissa, gave Victoria the word: "Nobody wears an everyday kilt to the Christmas concert!"

Of course I didn't hear about this right away. There was mostly silence until 5 P.M. Then this deteriorated into quiet sobs. Victoria is the kind of child who mentions a year later that there was a school play and she didn't get a part in it. Anyway, it was a miracle that by nine o'clock she finally sputtered out the truth, between Kleenexes: *Nobody wears an everyday kilt to the Christmas concert!*" What a gem! Tens of thousands of hardcover copies of *Timothy Goes to*

School, plus a paperback, not to mention British, French, German, Italian and Spanish editions, all trumpeting Melissa's *bon mot* to the world!

Melissa had made trouble since kindergarten. Today, in tenth grade, she's making more trouble. I could have told you then that she was destined to smoke at the age of thirteen. I've learned that kids like Melissa only get worse and more powerful. Also, they're not rolling stones — they never move away. They don't go and bother some other child in Tennessee. Anyway, when Victoria spilled the beans and this one glorious line I held her and rocked her in my arms.

"Never mind," I said. "Melissa probably didn't mean it."

"Oh, yes she did, she hates me!" Victoria said. "She never asked me to her birthday."

"You said you were just as glad, sweetie. You told me she locked Linda in the closet for three hours at the party."

"Yes, but she hates me, and today everybody heard her and everybody laughed at me."

"Maybe Melissa doesn't get enough love," I suggested.

"She has a pony," Victoria sobbed, "and ten different outfits from Saks Fifth Avenue."

"That isn't love," I said.

"Yes it is," said Victoria.

"Everyone will forget all about it after Christmas vacation," I told her.

"Then she'll say something else," Victoria answered. And of course she was right. So I didn't bother with any more discussion. I just gave her a bag of M & M's, which is a superb mood elevator because, unlike talk, it's neither cheap nor fake. That is why child psychologists shouldn't write or criticize or come near the field of children's books. They actually believe what they say.

Back to *Timothy Goes to School.*

Why are the characters raccoons and not people? They are animals because animals can do all sorts of things that kids would look overly cute doing, or overly cruel. Animals can jump out of trees and knock each other down, which of course happens to real kids, but it would take a better illustrator than I am to make such a scene palatable. Animals can also be superbly funny, where the same visual humor involving children would be slapstick. All the animals in my books, incidentally, are based on our West Highland white terrier, Angus. Born three years before our oldest daughter and resentful from her birth forward, that dog had more visible emotions than Elmer Gantry. He has been succeeded by other "westies," and each one is at least a Meryl Streep or a Laurence Olivier. Animals can live in a world that children seem to climb right into. It's a world of the past, with clothing from other times. Things aren't modern in the world of animals. Walter Gropius hasn't been born, or Arnold Schönberg, or Lee Iacocca. There are no color barriers, because animals come in all colors and no one minds. This world seems to suit my stories, and animals are easier for me to draw than people. Timothy happens to be a raccoon. He is also a boy, though Victoria is a girl, obviously. Why a boy? Because of the clothes. Boys are as sensitive about clothes as girls are, but if you make the lead characters girls in a book about a clothing fight, they come off as bitchy stereotypes. Boys come off funny and very real.

At the end of the book, after Timothy has battled the unyielding and implacable Claude until he can't stand it any longer, what happens? Well, what happened to Victoria? Nothing. She suffered until she simply outgrew Melissa and was in a different class. But years can't pass in a picture book. Things must be resolved. Fortunately, the device of *deus ex machina* is at my disposal. Almost every good writer uses it. In real life such quick fixes don't happen nearly often enough, but they must happen in children's books because the world wakes kids up in a cold sweat at 4 A.M. In fact, the world of school continues to do so even when they are forty and fifty. My worst nightmares are still those dreams in which I haven't gone to class and there's a final exam in an hour. Patty D'Amico, the bully of the kickball diamond, still lurks in my memory, and she resurrects every six months or so. So does Sue Ann Thompson, who was so beautiful that boys fell down in front of her, and Miriam Evans, valedictorian, who was so smart and so beautiful that girls, boys and teachers were her slaves.

It therefore took only a minute for me to absorb my Victoria's agony and to know how to write *Timothy Goes to School*. After that there were many occasions, like parents' night, when I wanted to go up to Melissa's mother and give her a piece of my mind. I would picture myself saying, "And what's more, it wouldn't surprise me one bit if Melissa developed a reputation for hiding in the bushes with boys in the seventh grade, and cheating on midterms in the ninth grade, and drinking beer by tenth grade" — all of which did come true, by the way. Of course I always held my tongue. But there is sweet revenge in this world after all. *Timothy* has sold steadily and

well for ten years now, and Victoria is in another
school — with another and bigger Melissa.

Just as there are universal emotions and predicaments
common to young childhood, so there are for teenagers as well. In some ways, to be fourteen now is no
different than it was for me or my mother. That part
of writing for teenagers is familiar to me, and having
those fragile and unstoppable joys and fears in my
grasp is where I start. On the other hand, the 1980s
and '90s are not like anything that has gone before.
The change in what young people value and what they
will become is staggering. It is the nuances of that
change that only *they* know truly, like a language. If
you're not in your teens, you can only imitate the
voice; you can't be there with them, because no adults
are allowed. They are on a bridge, these young people. They have stepped off the shore of the land
where they were safe with us. Some go early and
others follow late, but sooner or later they all must
walk across to the other side by themselves.

That's why they need each other's approval so des-
perately. This has always been so, of course — everybody has been on that bridge and, for better or worse,
has made it to the other shore. But now this journey
is made more perilous by the shills who are bombard-

ing our young people with ceaseless advertising. Sex, in its most infantile forms, is the loudest and most constant commodity. Too many young people are also dressing in black and taking very dangerous substances. They are saturated with glossy images of love, death and more material things than their money can buy. Often their families have melted away like snow in the sun, if they existed at all. It's not easy for these kids to have any sense of self. What I have chosen to write about in my next book is a journey under that bridge of a solitary youngster punting his own boat.

Writing a novel is like living next door to a family that has just moved in. At first you just see the people coming and going, in and out of their house. After a while their habits become more familiar, and then one day you go in for coffee. Soon you're invited for dinner, and before you know it you're there for Thanksgiving. By then you're a part of the family, and you know where they keep the good brandy and how early they get up to let the dog out. You're stuck. If there has been a death or an illness you suffer, or if there has been a murder you wake up in the dark scared to death. Writing a novel is just like that, except that you have made all the people up. But that doesn't matter, because by the time the novel is finished you're convinced that they are alive.

[56

At one point in my book *The Man in the Woods*, which gave me a lot of trouble, I told Phyllis, my editor, that since a great deal of the action is historically factual and involves a Civil War family in New Bedford, Massachusetts, I wanted to include old photographs of the family to illustrate the book. Phyllis told me that old photographs are the kiss of death in a teenage book and please not to do it. I was very stubborn. That summer I actually went out and scoured the antiques stores on Cape Cod for old photograph albums. I was searching for someone who looked like my character Lucy Fairchild. And I did find her — I swear I found Lucy's picture. She's a lovely, dignified woman, and obviously intelligent. I have that photograph framed. People ask who it is. I say, "That's Lucy Fairchild. She lived in New Bedford during the Civil War."

Other people's books are the greatest teachers of writers. Josephine Tey's *Miss Pym Disposes* is probably the most perfect mystery ever written. It's perfect in the sense that a Telemann oboe concerto is perfect; it's not a Mahler symphony. This book taught me that mystery stories can be splendid literature. There are no policemen in *Miss Pym Disposes*. The central character is a retired teacher who decides to visit an old classmate, a headmistress of a girls' prep school in the quiet English countryside. The girls are introduced one by one, or in groups. Their intrigues and souls are displayed gently. The life of the school, its place among other schools, its program and examinations are all explained with dry wit and unusual color. Before the reader knows it, the table is totally set — by page 100 exactly. Then, very suddenly, the sun goes in and this idyllic place becomes sinister in the light of someone's having cheated on an exam. Much depends on the results of these exams; girls' whole lives can turn on the jobs they get after school. An accidental death occurs, which only Miss Pym knows is not an accident.

There are no stolen jewels, secret formulas or packets of drugs in *Miss Pym Disposes;* only human nature at its most playful and complex. In the meantime we get a wonderful view of Josephine Tey's postwar England as it was lived by the upper middle class. The author's position is that the reader is a person with adequate education, which means, since the book is set in 1949, a positively brilliant education. This alone is enough to seduce a reader who is tired of mysteries that give every detail of a deranged massacre. Most books in this genre are also big on obligatory sex scenes, except those written by truly good writers like John le Carré and Dick Francis. Sex scenes in mystery books are like raw legs of lamb hurled into a lobster bisque.

I was so struck by the craft of *Miss Pym Disposes* that I made a chart of the plot. I used twelve different colored pens. Where were the clues hidden? Where was the structure turned from innocent to sinister? When did the sun go in? I showed the chart to Phyllis in the middle of writing *Leave Well Enough Alone*, which was my first mystery novel. She couldn't make head or tail of it. Never mind. The book went through six drafts; the next novel took four, the next one nine or ten.

Incidentally, I've intentionally emphasized my relationship with my editor. Editors are usually thanked at the end of a speech; they're seldom acknowledged as working partners. But all books need editors. When I read one that is overlong, or that has a part that's uneven or makes no sense, I don't ask what the author was doing, because I make all those mistakes myself. I do ask, "Where was the editor?" A book that is guided and preened and patted to perfection by a good editor is seamless. Before I start a novel I read John Cheever and Evan Connell. This sets the language right in my mind. When I finish, and when Phyllis has finished with it, it's the best I can do.

The next book and next family are now looming

over me. I hear their voices all the time. Two nights ago I was in the Grand Union, waiting in a checkout line. There was a woman ahead of me. The cashier dragged the woman's groceries over the little screen with the dancing red light that reads the price codes on the packages. The woman asked her, "How long have you been working here, honey?" "About a year," she said. The woman put her hand on the checker's arm, pointed to the screen with the red light and said, "Those things cause cancer in mice!" That woman walked right into my next book.

The most often asked question of all authors is where their ideas come from. It's answered in a variety of ways, not the least being, "It's my job to have ideas." But that's not a good enough answer. There is a "where," and it's not in any author's head. The closest I've ever heard anyone come to it was Peter Shaffer in the play *Amadeus*. The important idea in *Amadeus* has nothing to do with whether Salieri killed Mozart or whether Mozart was a profane fool. It has to do with the fact that Mozart heard the voices of angels. He had only to sit with score paper, and the music burst out from heaven into his head and down his arm and out of his pen. Lesser mortals — like Salieri, who wrote very nice pieces that are still played by classical music stations several lifetimes after his death — might not have heard angels, but their music also came from somewhere. Salieri thought it was God over his shoulder. Perhaps he was right.

I don't hear angels' voices either, but I do know that when my ordinary conscious self is gone, stories and characters — laughing and crying and doing all kinds of things — fill not my head but my writing screen. I believe that all stories and plays and paintings and songs and dances come from a palpable but unseen space in the cosmos. Ballets and symphonies written during our lifetime were there before we were born. According to how gifted we are, we are all given a large or small key to this treasury of wonders. I have been blessed with a small key to the world of the young. It's a place where good and evil are clearly stamped. It's a place where the better part of human nature triumphs over tragedies, and where innocence rides high. It is a great pleasure to write there, because the young have what the rest of us can only envy, and that is a belief in goodness and perpetual hope.

JILL KREMENTZ

Listening to Children

When I think back to when I was ten, it was such a different life from what a ten-year-old lives today. There was no television, so what I knew about the outside world came mostly from books like the Nancy Drew series and *The Secret Garden*. I wasn't reading books like the ones I now write; I don't think there *were* any books like that. I didn't know, for instance, that you could take ballet and get to be in *The Nutcracker* and grow up to be a dancer. I thought ballet was just something I had to take after school — it had no connection with anything I might ever do. What girls of my generation were reading, in other words, was fiction and fantasy, and I'm sure that all the work I've since done, as a photographer and as a writer, has been a rebellion against that. I've been determined that children reading books today won't grow up as deprived of reality as I was.

I'd like to tell you how some of my books got born, especially the "How It Feels" books: *How It Feels When a Parent Dies*, *How It Feels to Be Adopted*, *How It Feels When Parents Divorce* and the one I've just finished, *How It Feels to Fight for Your Life*, which is about children who are struggling with serious illnesses. I want to explain the process of how I choose and interview these many different kinds of children and why I think their stories are helpful to other children and their families.

I started working and having heroes almost simultaneously — when I was nineteen. My heroes (and they still continue to influence me) were Jacob Riis, Lewis Hine, Dorothea Lange and Gordon Parks — men and women who truly photographed *people* and did it with their heart. Of course they did it in a very artistic way; they had strong aesthetic values. But to me the main thing was that they helped to bring about change. They used their pictures not only to gather information but to put it to constructive use. I've never been someone who would want to take pretty pictures and hang them on the wall and that's the end of it. I've always wanted to channel what I gather — to reprocess information in a way that's helpful to others.

Another one of my early heroes was Margaret Mead. When I was a young reporter for *Time* magazine I took Dr. Mead's anthropology course at Columbia and I made a point of getting to know her. I think I realized very early that I wanted to do books about how people live. The course was basic anthropology, and that's what I've been doing ever since. What I like about anthropology is that it's nonjudgmental. In my "How It Feels" books, which deal with issues of loss that are highly complex — adoption, death, divorce, serious illness — I try to present every side of the issue without taking any side myself. What I learned from Margaret Mead was to be relentless and persistent in what I was going after, to work very hard and to be a good listener.

That course was the jumping-off point for my career as a writer of children's books. It began with a book called *Sweet Pea*, which is about a nine-year-old black girl growing up in Alabama in the 1960s. Originally I intended *Sweet Pea* to be part of a series, a group of books about different subcultures within the United States. I wanted to do an Amish child, and a child living in the bayou country, and an Indian child on a reservation. As it turned out, I didn't do the series because my editor left Harcourt Brace. In fact, looking back, I think I was lucky even to get *Sweet Pea* published. It's my own favorite of all my books, but now it wouldn't be commercial enough; publishers in the juvenile field today have their eye on the bottom line. But I have no doubt about the value that such a series could have had, because the more we understand different lifestyles within our own country the better off we all are.

Sweet Pea came about because I was doing a story for *Pageant* magazine about the Job Corps in Poland Springs, Maine. They had sent me to photograph a young girl who had three roommates, one of whom was a black girl named Emma who lived in Mount Meigs, Alabama. I had become very involved in the civil rights movement. As a staff photographer for the *New York Herald Tribune* I had covered the funeral of the three young men who were killed in 1964 in Mississippi: Andrew Goodman, Michael Schwerner and James Earl Chaney. I had also covered the riots in Harlem, in Bedford-Stuyvesant and in Newark. I cared deeply about the issue, and I wanted to go south like Walker Evans and Margaret Bourke-White and Erskine Caldwell and see what was going on.

I asked Emma if she could show me around if I came down. When I asked her if there was a hotel near where she lived, she said, "Well, it would really be easier if you stayed with us." So I did, for about a week, and I was very impressed with Emma's little sister, Sweet Pea. When I came home I was looking at all my pictures, and the pictures of Sweet Pea struck me as especially strong and good. Just at that time I was on a television program, and I showed my pictures there, and the writer Maggie Paley saw them and put me in touch with an editor at Harcourt Brace. She agreed to publish the book, and I went back to Mount Meigs to stay with the family three different times, including Christmas. And that's how I got to be a writer of children's books.

My method is the same with every book. I take along two cameras (a Leica M-6 and a Nikon), a tape recorder and a small spiral notebook. The notebook is for my field notes. It's never enough to just take pictures and to tape-record what a child says; I also need to know what the child was doing and observing and thinking and feeling, and what the people around him or her were thinking and saying. Then I convert all that information into a first-person narrative. A small example would be my book *Zachary*

Goes to the Zoo. The curator is touring the zoo with us, and I'm photographing Zachary looking at the giraffe, but I might see a sign explaining that a giraffe has four stomachs and a tongue one foot long, and I'll write that down in my notes and then have Zachary say it.

During this process I think of myself as the reader and try to make sure I understand the situation. I assume that if *I* understand it, any six-year-old will. It's a big advantage that I've approached most of my subjects not knowing anything about them. When I started working on *A Very Young Rider* and was attending my first horse shows, I'd be standing there asking the person next to me which end of the horse was supposed to go over the jump first. They'd tell me, and then they'd ask, "What brings you here?" and I'd explain that I was writing a book about horseback riding.

Certainly all my friends thought it was hilarious that I was writing. a cookbook. But I think it may be one of the best cookbooks, because it doesn't take anything for granted. It not only lists the ingredients you'll need; it lists every utensil. But the main reason I'm fond of my cookbook is that I think cooking is wonderful for kids. It teaches them math; it teaches them to share; it gives them control; they get quick results; and they learn to do something they can do

[70

well. It's also a lot of fun — that's why I call it *The Fun of Cooking* — and it's noncompetitive. Children today are under far too much competitive stress, even in their after-school activities. I don't want my daughter to do stressful things when the school day is over.

In my field notes I'm also on the lookout for feelings. In *A Very Young Gymnast,* when I was photographing Torrance, there were many times when I didn't want to intrude on the moment any more than was necessary. Therefore I made a draft of what I thought she might have been feeling at the time — in her own words. Then I went over it with her later, so that she could correct it or substitute words of her own. The final text went like this: "When the rips on my palms bleed, I cry because it hurts so much. Once in a while I cry because I'm just so tired and nothing seems to go right."

All the children in my books have the final right of approval. I feel very strongly about that. Some people are surprised — they think it's unprofessional. But I feel the same way about my books that I feel about my photography: that it's a collaboration between me and the person I'm working with. If I photograph someone, I want to use photographs that will please him.

After I go over the copy with the child and we've

71]

got what we think is good, we let his parents see it. I do this because it would be too easy to exploit children; they're extremely honest. The reason you get them to say such wonderful things is that they don't edit themselves if they trust you, and you can't violate that trust. Also, it's one thing to *talk* about your parents, but when children see what they've said in black and white and realize that it's going to be in a book, they may want to soften their remarks a little. I don't want these kids to hurt anybody. Also, I have to get the mother and father to sign off; that's a legal requirement because I'm dealing with minors. Fortunately, no parent has ever refused to sign; it's usually a question of some factual detail. They call up and say, "We have a few changes," and my heart is in my stomach. Then they say I've got it wrong about how old their dog is.

I think the reason parents are willing to stand by the material — even though it's often threatening to them — is that they respect what I'm trying to do. They all wish there had been the kind of book I was writing when *they* needed it, a year earlier. As a result, the "How It Feels" books are now what some-one gives somebody else who is in the same situation. Last year in Florida I met a delightful little girl named Samantha, who was swimming in the hotel pool with her mother and talking to my six-year-old daughter, Lily. I made a mental note to send her a copy of my book *Lily Goes to the Playground* when we all got back to New York. A month later her mother called me, sobbing. She said that her husband had died of a heart attack the previous day and that Samantha's school had sent home a copy of *How It Feels When a Parent Dies*. "I never imagined that the first book of yours I'd read would be this one," she said. What the book did was to enable her to know what her daughter would be thinking, because Samantha was only five and couldn't really articulate her thoughts. One important thing the mother was able to find out immediately, for instance, was that she probably should involve Samantha in the funeral.

Let me explain how I happened to get started doing these books. A friend of mine, Audrey Maas, died suddenly and unexpectedly after a short illness. She and her husband, Peter, and their little boy, John Michael, who was only eight, lived near us in the country, and in the days after Audrey's funeral we would go over and visit the house. I noticed that Peter had friends who had gone through a similar experience. But John Michael seemed very isolated, with nobody to talk to. So I thought it might be nice to try to do a book for other kids who are going through this. It would help them to know that some of the weird feelings they were having weren't inappropriate. For instance, I had heard that John Michael told someone that he didn't understand why, right after his mother died, this perpetual cocktail party was going on. He had no way of knowing that such gatherings are a kind of grieving ritual that almost all societies have. But the only children's books that I had seen on this subject were about kids who had lost a grandparent, or maybe a gerbil. Obviously, many children had lost a parent, and that's what I decided to focus on.

Because I had done six books that focused on *one* child — *Sweet Pea* and the five "Very Young" books — my first thought was to follow one young girl through the death of her mother, probably of cancer, so that I would be on hand when it happened. I just assumed that a mother's death would be a bigger loss than the death of a father. But then I had second thoughts. Statistically, probably more children are losing fathers, because many fathers have heart attacks and they're usually older than their wife. Would my book help a little boy whose father dies? I also wondered what religion I should use. If I had an Episcopalian funeral, would it be relevant for a

Jewish child? And how about the burial — should it be in a cemetery, or would the parent be cremated? Should the child have siblings, or should he or she be an only child? And I hadn't even thought about suicide, which is a surprisingly frequent cause of death among relatively young people. I realized that I would have to think more broadly.

At about that time I was asked to give a talk about my "Very Young" books to a group of librarians in Westchester County, New York. I told them about my project and read them a few passages by the children I had begun to interview. I asked them if they knew of any children in their schools who had lost a parent and who might like to participate. Within a week I had heard from eight of those librarians, and they all had wonderful kids for me; librarians are really in touch with the kids in their schools. And children who like to read have always been my best subjects. That's probably because they realize the value of books for themselves and for others. I also put a notice in my alumni magazine and called the Big Brother organization. In the case of two of the children, Nick Davis and Susan Radin, their mothers had been close friends of mine before they died. Pretty soon I had the eighteen boys and girls I ended up using.

I pick my children carefully — I don't just go out and find eighteen children who have had a parent die. I look for an age range from six to sixteen; at seventeen you're moving into an adult book. In fact, I don't have that many who are sixteen, or six — just one or two. I want to be able to reach down to the six-year-olds, and if there's one six-year-old in the book, they feel that they have a friend they can latch on to. But after that I'm going for a median age. I want the book fairly evenly divided between girls and boys. I also want certain demographics — some blacks and Hispanics and Mexicans, not just little white children. I want both Christian and Jewish kids. I want some children who have brothers and sisters and some who don't; I want children who have been helped by psychiatrists and children who hate psychiatrists.

Most of all, I want a range of issues. My books are designed to show both sides of every question. In *How It Feels When Parents Divorce*, for instance, there are various custody arrangements. There's one family where the mother and the father moved in and out and the child stayed in the house; there were arrangements where the mother had sole custody and the child never saw the father; where the father had sole custody and the mother disappeared; where the children switched back and forth every other night, or every six months. I wanted to include a wide variety of possible structures. In *How It Feels to Be Adopted* I wanted it pretty evenly divided on the issue of "to search or not to search" for the birth parent, and also to cover children who had been searched *for*. My own opinion doesn't enter into it; nobody reading these books would know where I stand. In fact, that book was embraced by both the "search" faction and the "don't search" faction. They all gave me quotes and felt that the book was fair and evenhanded — which pleased me, because both groups are very strident.

I tried for the same diversity in *How It Feels When a Parent Dies*. Of the eighteen children, probably half want to go to the cemetery on Easter and Christmas, and the other half never want to go because it gives them the heebie-jeebies and just reminds them of their own mortality, or it makes them worry that something will happen to their surviving parent. But on one issue — whether or not the child should go to the parent's funeral — without exception the children who went to the funeral were glad and the ones who didn't go regretted it later, because even if they were too young to know that they hadn't gone, when they got older they found out and felt that they should have been there. I feel very strongly about that issue, and I think it's one of the most important lessons that can be drawn from any of my books.

Another lesson, which took me by surprise, was how many children were comforted by an open casket, because in my own life that was never a part of any funeral I attended. But to these kids who had lost a parent it made death more concrete and real. It enabled them to understand, because they were so young, that the parent had in fact died. They could see the dead parent and could sense that the soul had somehow left the body. It was different from sleeping; grown-ups often say to children, "She's gone to sleep forever," but that's confusing, because when people go to sleep they wake up. One of the kids in the book, Gardner Harris, puts it like this:

"I just couldn't realize her death until a few days later when I saw her dead in the open casket. That was one of her last wishes — to have an open casket. . .˙. I saw the shell of what had been my mother, but it wasn't my mother lying there. It was then that I realized that my mother had been using that body while she was alive, but that the real person, the person I loved who was Mom, was somewhere else and would never die. Her spirit was part of me and part of all of us. If I died and I had children

I would want to have an open casket too, because it would help them realize that even if I died I would always be a part of them."

But there was one experience even worse for children than having a parent die. Divorce — as I found out when I was writing *How It Feels When Parents Divorce* — is the most painful of the traumas that my books deal with. Yet it's the most underestimated of all the injurious things that happen to children. Parents put blinders on, and by the time they finally get the divorce they have convinced themselves that they did it for the sake of the children. They also look at the statistics and say, "Divorce is so common; the kids'll survive; they all survive." The parents think of it as like chicken pox — just something children go through. They'll be uncomfortable for a little while, but they'll soon feel better.

What makes a divorce so long lasting in its effects has to do with self-image and ego. If a parent dies, he or she is all but deified by the surviving parent. It's always, "Oh, your father would have been so proud of you," or "Your father was such a wonderful man," or "You're just as pretty as your mother was." It's a positive reinforcement of the missing parent, which, while it may sadden the child on one level, makes the child feel good about himself. Also, there's no fighting. The child of a divorce is told that the reason mommy and daddy are separating is that they're fighting all the time, but that after the divorce they're not going to fight anymore. In fact, the fighting is just beginning, but it's done in a more insidious way. Even in a "civilized" divorce, for example, it's not unusual to have one parent say to the child, "You'd better call your father and remind him to pick you up on Saturday." That seems like a fairly benign remark, and the mother is proud that she put it so nicely. But the implication is that the father doesn't care enough to remember.

Logistically, too, divorce is hard for children because there's far more joint custody today — at a time when there are more working mothers and children are doing more after-school activities than ever before. When I was young you came home and you had a peanut butter and jelly sandwich and you went out and played. You could play at this house or you could play at that house. Now there's ballet class one day and gymnastics or skating the next, and all these activities require accouterments, like ice skates and sneakers and leotards, so that the kids never have what they need where they need it. One little girl in my book says, "Two rooms of one's own does not add up to one room of one's own." She felt very disoriented. These kids also hate going on the class list — the list that's on every family's refrigerator door, with the names and addresses of the children and their parents. In fact, that's often the first question they ask: "Do you have to put it on the class list?"

With *How It Feels to Be Adopted,* I was surprised by how many parents turned me down. Many of them felt they had gone very far by even telling their children they were adopted. I always approach the parents first; I don't want to ask the children first and have them want to do it and then find their parents opposed, so that the parents become the bad guys. My ideal subject is therefore the child of a parent who, when I say I'm working on the project, says, "Well, I know Melissa loved *A Very Young Dancer* — in fact, it's grafted onto her chest, she's been carrying it around so much. It's fine with me, but why don't you call *her,* because the decision is totally hers." Then I feel that I'm home free, because, first, that's the kind of parent who lets her child make decisions like that, and, second, it's a parent who allows her child to have her own feelings. The opposite extreme is the parent who says, "If you were to interview Katie it would just open up a whole Pandora's box." That's the child I worry about for years afterward. I can always get enough children to interview, but *that* child would have benefited the most from talking about her feelings, and if the parents are already thinking of adoption as a Pandora's box, then it surely is one.

I believe that all the children in my books have benefited from the experience. Often their teachers have told me how much better they're doing in school, or the children have written me themselves. They were so proud to be in a book, as well they might be; it makes *me* proud that they were included just for being articulate and in touch with their feelings and not because they made the baseball team or got all A's.

Therefore one value of these books is that they enable children to listen to themselves. But their real value, I think, is that they enable children to listen to other children — to realize, often for the first time, that they are not alone in their situation. One little boy in *How It Feels When a Parent Dies*, Nick Davis, says he asked himself, about a month after his mother died, "If it had to happen over again, would it have been better to have Dad die? I didn't really answer the question because I felt so guilty even thinking it." Another child reading that passage might have had the same thought and yet, discussing it with his mother or father, might say, "Boy, can you believe that kid said such an awful thing?" And you hope it's the wise and perceptive parent who says, "Of course I can. In fact, I'd be surprised if you didn't think that yourself sometimes; it would be only natural." Right away that parent has given his child permission to think what he probably thought was unthinkable.

The most important thing I learned from doing this book came from Carla Lehman, age eleven. She told me that what bothered her most after her father died was when people would say, "Oh, your father was such a wonderful man. I knew him from before you were born." That's exactly what *I* would have told a young child whose parents I had known well. And it's exactly what made Carla feel worst, because she was so angry and jealous of that person who had known her father longer. "Lots of people came over to the house," she said, "but I didn't want to talk to anybody who had more memories of my father than I had." What adults don't realize is that children who lose a parent feel very threatened by the fact that they knew that parent such a short time. They worry that they have too few memories and that they're even going to lose *them*. They want to talk about that parent a lot; they want pictures around. They're scared that if they just keep everything in their memory bank, they might push the wrong button and wake up some morning and find that all their memories have been erased.

Finally, I'd like to tell you about the book I've just finished, *How It Feels to Fight for Life*, which seemed like the natural fourth in the series. It's been by far the hardest and most painful one to write. I'm dealing with children who have fourteen different illnesses and disabilities: three kinds of cancer (aplastic anemia, leukemia and osteogenic sarcoma), open-heart surgery, cystic fibrosis, multiple burns (from a homemade chemistry experiment that blew up in the boy's face), spinal injury (a boy, shot in the spine, who is now a paraplegic and an outstanding wheelchair athlete), spina bifida, lupus, epilepsy, diabetes, asthma, juvenile rheumatoid arthritis and kidney failure.

Actually, it's not the illnesses that I've focused on. I'm dealing primarily with the issues that the children are coping with — sibling rivalry, overprotective parents, financial stresses in the family, religious doubts, pain, hope, doctors who don't always listen to them, their relationships with schoolmates and their struggle for independence at a time when illness makes them more dependent than ever on their parents. One prob-

lem, for example, is that there's no privacy. I was at a
hospital one day, interviewing the boy with cystic
fibrosis. I was sitting beside his bed with my notes and
my tape recorder; we were clearly having what looked
like a serious meeting. I'll bet we were interrupted
ten times by hospital people walking into the room,
not to give him medication but just interrupting. All
the children I've interviewed talk about how inva-
sive this is. The psychiatrist drops in and expects
them to spill their guts. The chaplain walks in to
say hello. The children don't feel that they have
any rights.

I hope this book is going to be particularly helpful to doctors. Good doctors are eager to know what
these kids are feeling, especially if someone else —
someone like me — can do some of the listening for
them. They're so overworked that they don't have
time to sit down and just talk to their young patients.
Whenever I'm at the hospital the doctors are scream-
ing into a phone trying to get blood work done, or
using their lunch hour to go down and prod someone in the x-ray department. What *I'm* trying to
focus on are quality-of-life issues. They may not be
medically related to the illness, but they're deeply
related to the recovery.

As for the medical issues, that's why the book has

taken me twice as long as the other three "How It Feels" books. When I worked on the divorce book I at least knew what a divorce was; we all know that. But these illnesses are unfamiliar — you can't begin to interview a child until you've read the literature. (And medical literature is a language unto itself.) Before I could understand the problems that a child with lupus has, or a child with juvenile rheumatoid arthritis, I had to understand the disease, so that I would know what problems we were talking about. Are they diseases that require children to take a lot of medicine? If so, I want to know how this affects their life and what the physical effects of the medicine are, because those happen to be two diseases where the treatment itself is life-threatening. In the case of cancer, I already knew about nausea and the loss of hair from chemotherapy. But I never knew about the mouth sores, and this is as gigantic a problem as the other two. It's certainly something you want to talk about in a book that other children with the same illness will read; it will make them better prepared, psychologically, when they start treatment themselves. Most of the children I interviewed felt that they had a higher threshold for pain when they knew what to expect. Yet a doctor may not even mention mouth sores. Doctors often tend to minimize pain. So when children do have these adverse reactions they think there's something terribly wrong, and their anxiety triggers a bad response all around.

I chose the title *How It Feels to Fight for Your Life* because it puts the child in an active, positive role. Even if the illness isn't literally life-threatening, what all these children are still fighting for is a normal life — one that is ennobled and that has a dignity they want and can reach for. My point is not to talk about a particular disease, or to tell people what it's like to be sick. I'm using children who I hope will be role models for other children. I'd like some other girl with rheumatoid arthritis to read about ten-year-old Lauren Dutton and say, "I don't really like playing the piano, but I like it enough so that if it's going to be good for my joints and make my fingers exercise, that's more interesting than the dumb exercises I'm doing with my therapist, and I might even learn to play the piano, too."

There's one young boy in my book, Spencer Gray, who had a kidney transplant. He's terrific. He can't do contact sports, and he's also quite small because all the steroids have stunted his growth, so he signed up with the ROTC program at school. I went to photograph him in his uniform, and this is what he told me: "Master Gunny Washington, who works with our group, told me right off to stop worrying about my size and not to think of myself as a novelty. What he said was, 'Size doesn't mean anything — it's the size of your heart that matters.' I go to training every day at 7:30, and on Tuesdays and Thursdays I have a drill at eight o'clock. We've won the city championship four years in a row. When I go to ROTC I forget that I'm smaller than the other kids, and a lot of the time I even forget that I'm sick. All I feel is real proud."

JEAN FRITZ

The Teller and the Tale

I don't think it's possible to discuss the craft of writing for children without first exploring the nature of the writer. I suspect that anyone who writes — particularly those who write for children — had a childhood that for one reason or another was very vivid. Often it was also a lonely childhood, with solitude enough to expand one's capacity for wonder, to sharpen awareness, to encourage remembrance. My own childhood was spent in China, and it has lived with me ever since. Indeed, I can't remember a time when I didn't think that the world was a great deal stranger and harder to explain than my missionary parents let on.

Isaiah Berlin, drawing on an old Greek quotation,

divided people into two categories: hedgehogs and foxes. Hedgehogs are those who want to change the world, who try to fit it into a single, overall explanation. Foxes, on the other hand, accept the world as it is, exulting in all its variety and its paradoxes and its many explanations, or even its lack of explanation. That may be a simplistic notion, but, in any case, there were a lot of hedgehogs around in my childhood. I heard men exchange stories of when they "heard the call," in the same way that women trade descriptions of having a baby. I had no idea what the call was. But I lived in terror that one day I would hear the call myself.

I needn't have worried, for, as I discovered much later, I was not susceptible. I was a fox, listening, savoring, observing, first trying out life as one person and then as another, exulting in the diversity of the world. And in China there was plenty of diversity. Like most people who become writers, I was unconsciously storing away this personal material. Yet when I actually started writing it was fiction that I wrote, fiction set in American history.

I needed to accumulate a long American past for my displaced childhood. That much I realized. Nor was I surprised that I was writing for young people. What I didn't recognize until much later was that I was also trying, in a disguised form, to work out past and present personal relationships.

With my fourth novel, *Early Thunder*, however, I suddenly became impatient with the fictional framework. The story was set in Salem, Massachusetts, a year before the Revolution broke out, and my research turned up such incredible events in that year that I longed to tell the story as it actually happened. But in fiction everything depends on the illusion of reality. And so, to maintain that illusion, I had to tone down the reality, and it was such a waste of good material.

At this point I decided to move straight into nonfiction — into biography, where I would be caught up in the life of a real person and where, however strange the events, I could just let 'er rip! I would make up nothing, not even the dialogue, and I wouldn't even use dialogue unless I had a source. I would be honest. If there was a fact I wasn't sure of, or if it was unknown, I would say so.

I started with Paul Revere, perhaps because as a child I felt uncomfortable with Longfellow. I always felt that Longfellow was trying to take me on his lap, to make sure I would listen and hear *his* midnight story of Paul Revere. But when *I* told the story of Paul I wanted to jump into specific, unexpected facts, the kind that give the past a pulse. Fortunately, I had just found in a small, second-hand bookstore Justin Winsor's wonderful four-volume *Memorial History of Boston*, with exactly the kind of minute details that I treasure. So I began. "In 1735," I wrote,

there were in Boston 42 streets, 36 lanes, 22 alleys, 1,000 brick houses, 2,000 wooden houses, 12 churches, 4 schools, 418 horses (at the last count), and so many dogs that a law was passed prohibiting people from having dogs that were more than 10 inches high.

There were, of course, people in Boston — more than 13,000. Four of them lived in a small wooden house on North Street near Love Lane. They were Mr. Revere, a gold and silversmith; his wife, Deborah; their daughter Deborah; and their young son Paul Revere, born the first day of the new year.

I called the book *And Then What Happened, Paul Revere?* It turned out to be sixty-four pages, as did my subsequent books about people in the Revolution. All of them have titles that are in the form of a question, because questions imply surprise. We underestimate the power of surprise in education. It seems to me that I have been surprised into learning almost everything I know.

As for the style of writing, I'm constantly asked,

"How do you know what children will like?" All I can say is, "Well, *I* was a child." I don't expect all children to react in the same way, but I write as if I'm talking to children, naturally. I limit my vocabulary, but not any more consciously than I do when I'm talking to my grandchildren. If you're intent on communicating, the vocabulary takes care of itself.

But I won't omit words because they may be strange to a young reader. In my research on Paul Revere, for instance, I had discovered Paul's own account of his midnight ride. He reported verbatim the talk between him and the British soldiers who stopped him. One soldier said, "Sir, may I crave your name?" Well, I relish that eighteenth-century use of the word "crave," and I wasn't going to take it out. I thought children could surely figure out its meaning from the context. There was another officer, however, who wasn't so polite. He said, "Damn you, stop! If you go an inch farther you are a dead man." I had no intention of meddling with that officer's words either.

But soon after the book was published I discovered that the world of education is filled with hedgehogs. Don't think I'm putting down hedgehogs; in every century great hedgehogs have moved the world forward. Usually it's the prickly, small-minded variety that hold the world back. They don't inhabit the world of trade books; it's the world of textbooks where they hang out, their red pencils at the ready. These prickly hedgehogs are particularly sensitive to the study of American history. They aren't interested in stimulating children to understand American history. They want to convince children in the easiest possible way that the past was perfect. When they reprinted my story of Paul Revere they decided that "crave" was a confusing word. "Damn" was absolutely unacceptable.

One group of Texas hedgehogs complained that I had demeaned an American hero when I said that Paul Revere seldom made a mistake in arithmetic. How could I imply that he *ever* made a mistake? They were incensed that I said Paul Revere doodled in his account book. If I had been patriotic I would have covered for him. Well, I don't have to accept a hedgehog's request for a hedge. And usually I don't.

Of course I do like my characters to make it into the schoolroom. In my so-called younger biographies, like *Paul Revere*, I zero in on the main characteristic of my subject. This immediately puts the reader on a familiar footing with the character, and it gives me a chance to match my narrative voice to the thrust of the material. Paul Revere, for instance, was one of those compulsively busy, active men, into everything,

[96

rushing from one project to another. So I assume a rather breathless style for his story — short sentences, long accumulated sentences that race from comma to comma, broken phrases, questions to move the story along quickly.

Although my framework is chronological, I don't feel bound by chronology. I can begin a series of sentences with "once" or "sometimes," listing events regardless of their sequence. I know that in the end the book will assume the shape of a story, not because it has been forced or coaxed into that, but because the story is already there. Every person is a story. And when a writer lives with a character, the story line emerges, gradually becoming more distinct, until at last it takes command. This is not to say that the writer follows effortlessly in its wake. One of the built-in hazards of this trade is the sleepless nights that accompany the period of composition. For some reason the horizontal position seems to prevent the motors from stopping.

It was on one of those sleepless nights that I decided to write some longer biographies, in addition to the short ones, so that I could explore my characters in more depth. The writer of biographies for adults and the writer of books for children or young people have much in common, especially their methods of research. But in the selection of a subject the writer for young people has both more freedom and more restrictions. If I were writing a biography for adults I probably wouldn't consider someone whose life had already been definitively treated, or who had been covered in recent years, unless I had a new angle — some brand new source material such as letters suddenly discovered in a faraway attic, which of course is every writer's dream. But biographies for young people, until quite recently, have often been so hagiographic, or didactic, or patronizing, or just plain dull that I have no shortage of people to choose from; I'm not so limited. On the other hand, some subjects are simply more appropriate for adults. I did write an adult biography — of Mercy Otis Warren, an eighteenth-century woman writer, a historian of the American Revolution and a worrying mother. I identified with her on all counts. But I couldn't have made her story accessible to young people.

When I started writing longer biographies I decided on certain guidelines. I would pick characters with dramatic, perhaps adventurous lives. They would also be people that I myself would be curious about, people whose personalities would require some unraveling. Their lives would be fairly well documented, and they would be people who could make it into the schoolroom. But in the end, how do you really decide and settle on one person? Children are always asking me that, and I have to say that I don't feel that I'm picking a person; I have the feeling that my subjects are picking *me*. This may sound suspiciously as if I am hearing "the call." All I mean is that I can't write on demand, or even make a calculated decision. The historian Peter Gay once said that every biography is part of a writer's autobiography, and I believe that. Something about a personality in the past commands a personal response in the present. Not admiration, necessarily; not love. Often, in fact, the relationship that I develop is a love/hate relationship. I grapple with a person as one sometimes does with a member of one's own family, in an attempt to reach a kind of understanding and arrive at acceptance.

Certainly I grappled with Stonewall Jackson — as eccentric, as rigid, as difficult a man as you could find. I sensed the ambition that drove him through his life, which he adamantly refused to acknowledge because his religion required him to sublimate himself to God. I felt sure that this basic paradox caused the anguish behind his character, but I needed a witness, a contemporary witness, to back me up. I searched long and hard, and then one day I met General Richard Taylor of Louisiana. Observing Stonewall Jackson closely, General Taylor wrote: "I caught a glimpse of the man's inner nature. It was but a glimpse, yet in that moment I saw an ambition boundless as Cromwell's, and as merciless. His ambition was vast, all-absorbing. He loathed it, perhaps feared it, but he could not escape it, it was himself. . . . He fought it with prayer, constant and earnest."

I started my book with a question I asked myself: How could such a compulsive, literal-minded oddball as Stonewall Jackson ever have become a national hero, not only famous for his military exploits but idolized in the way that rock stars are today? I guess the answer is, he got what he needed: a war. It suited him as nothing ever had or probably would have. And if I had been a soldier in his army, I would have loved him too, not in spite of his idiosyncrasies but because of them.

Then there were Sam Houston and Benedict Arnold. Sam fascinated me, but he didn't win me over until his old age, when he stepped down as governor of Texas rather than sign up with Jefferson Davis in the Confederacy. Here was a man with an ego as big as Texas itself. But he believed in the Union, and for the sake of principle he retired from the public stage that he was so very fond of. Benedict Arnold never won me over, but how I pitied him. The son of the town drunk, harassed as a boy by his peers, he determined at an early age that he would overcome life by being brave. He would be a hero; he would show the world. It's heartbreaking to see how truly brave he was and how great was his need to prove himself. Unfortunately, there was no room left in his makeup for judgment or morality. He never believed that he had done wrong; he simply believed what he wanted to believe, which is a fairly common human characteristic that has again and again led people and nations astray. Anyway, these were all adventurous men whose lives conformed to the guidelines I had set myself.

But two people were so compelling that I took them on regardless of the fact that they didn't meet all my requirements. One was Pocahontas. How could I resist this high-spirited girl, truly trapped between two cultures? Yet she left no personal record; her life would have to be pieced together, her emotions deduced from reading about Indians at that time, from reading accounts of the Jamestown settlers, especially John Smith's. Still, in the end, I did feel that I knew Pocahontas. But for lack of evidence I sometimes had to resort to such words as "may have," "must have" and "perhaps." Equally interesting to me when I was working on the book was the insight it gave me into the settlers themselves. Their accounts reveal in graphic terms their unbelievable arrogance toward the Native Americans. To read these records is to see the havoc that the white man has wreaked in so many parts of the world. When my daughter read my book about Pocahontas she said she could see that my childhood in China had participated in the writing.

As for the subject of my latest book, James Madison, I suspect that my need to write about him also had deep personal roots, although at first I had no intention of having anything to do with him. I originally met him when I was writing about the Constitutional Convention, and suddenly there he was at my elbow. "I'm next," he said. I looked him over — shy, awkward, without a single adventure in his life. "No," I told him, "you won't do." But he was insistent. "The Constitution had a hard time making it," he said. "Don't stop your story with the Convention." The more I thought about it, the more I realized that the essence of the American experiment was at the core of Madison's life. Certainly America had some very rocky years during his lifetime. All I had to do was to thread the story of this totally committed man through the life of the country itself, and I would have all the adventure, the suspense, the upheavals I needed. And

[102

I was given one extra piece of luck. If the city of Washington ever had to be burned, I was grateful that it was burned during Madison's administration.

But behind the story itself, *I* was there — a child who longed to feel like a real American. I wanted to give this very real American, Madison, a chance to have his say. Indeed, I needed him to speak to me. I knew the outline of his life and times, but it is only as a biographer travels slowly from year to year, making connections, that he or she comes into possession of a chunk of history. It seemed important that I come to the point of assimilating America's experiment at the moment when nobody was sure that it was going to work. Many people were skeptical and some frankly hoped they could send the Constitution back to the drawing board and start over from scratch. I was struck by a letter that James Madison wrote his father in the beginning of Washington's administration. "We are in a wilderness," he said, "without a single footstep to guide us. Those who may follow will have an easier task." Notice that he used the word "may," indicating that even in his own mind there was a question of whether the venture would succeed. I wanted to share in this period of uneasiness.

There is a misconception on the part of many adults, I think, about the process of writing history for children. They assume that it's just a matter of retelling well-known facts in simpler terms. Partly, perhaps. But there is seldom a time in my research when I don't run into a problem that I've never seen dealt with in a book, or a statement that doesn't need questioning. In my book on Benedict Arnold, for instance, I met a Revolutionary patriot named John Brown, who hated Arnold with such a consuming hatred that it twisted his life. I couldn't help but suspect that in addition to his known grievances he had some deep, personal grievance against Arnold. On the surface he had many obvious reasons. Brown was one of Ethan Allen's boys who resented Arnold's trying to take command in the capture of Fort Ticonderoga. He blamed Arnold for refusing to promote him in the Canadian expedition. And when Brown's brother died from an inoculation against smallpox, Brown said it was Arnold's fault for ordering inoculation throughout the army.

Eventually Brown did get his promotion. Still, he never gave up his ambition to bring Arnold down. He drew up a list of complaints and not only submitted it to the Continental Congress, but went from general to general in an attempt to get action. He got nowhere. And in his anger he resigned from the army and had a handbill printed, which he posted publicly. At the end of all its accusations he stated, "Money is this man's god, and to get enough of it he would sacrifice his country." Brown had reason to hate Arnold, but to hate him to that extent? Enough to assert such an extravagant claim?

When I discovered that Brown was married to a cousin of Arnold's I suspected a family grudge that ran beneath the professional ones. Arnold was known to have taken financial advantage of members of his family, and I tried to track something down, consulting all kinds of records, going to Pittsfield, Massachusetts, Brown's hometown. I found nothing. But I did give John Brown a larger role in my story than he is often given, and I made a connection that I hadn't seen made before. I imagined his "I told you so" reaction when he heard that Benedict Arnold had defected, so I looked up his whereabouts at the time. John Brown was in the Mohawk Valley fighting Indians, and I'm sorry to report that he was killed before he could hear the news.

When I was working on Pocahontas I came across a new theory by a historian so eminent that I couldn't overlook it. Yet if I accepted his theory, it would change the entire way I told my story, and it seemed to me to defy all common sense. He suggested that Pocahontas's uncle, a major character in the story, might have been the same Indian who was captured by the Spaniards many years earlier, taken to Spain for eight years, brought back to the Jamestown area by Jesuits and turned over to his own tribe in the hope that he would convert them to Christianity. Instead he and his tribe killed the Jesuits. At this point, according to the eminent historian, the uncle took a new name for himself, Opechancanough, which supposedly meant "he whose soul is white." None of the settlers mentioned that Opechancanough showed any knowledge of European ways or passed any of this information on to his people, yet many of the Indians were close to the settlers and had made friends with them. If Opechancanough had seen European cities, why wouldn't he have stopped his brother, Powhatan, from giving his emissary to England a stick, with instructions to cut a notch on it for every person he saw, so that he could figure out the population of England? Or why would Opechancanough as an old man have asked the settlers to build him an English house, and, when it was built, have spent his days walking in and out of the front door, entranced by the magic of the front door key? If he had been in Spain for eight years, surely he would have seen a key; he wouldn't have been knocked out by the act of locking and unlocking a door.

It didn't make sense, but I know that life can be

bizarre, so I checked at the Library of the American Indian in Chicago. The people there had also heard this theory, but they were as skeptical as I was. They gave me the name of a leading authority on Jamestown. In fact, he lived in Jamestown. I went to him, and he also knew about the theory and dismissed it out of hand. Finally I called the Smithsonian Institution's authority on Native American languages to ask him about the translation of "Opechancanough." Could it mean "he whose soul is white"? His anwer was unequivocal: the language of Pocahontas's people had been lost. Besides, there's no word in any Native American language to correspond to our word "soul."

I would be disappointed if writing history for young people didn't raise such tantalizing questions for me to ponder. But the real incentive for the writer comes from the drive not only to know but to incorporate another time into oneself — to penetrate that time and that person's psychology in such a way that it will forever be a part of his or her total response to life.

The writer is on a quest. I. F. Stone, in the introduction to his book *The Trial of Socrates*, describes his own motivation. "The more I fell in love with the Greeks," he says, "the more agonizing grew the spectacle of Socrates before his judges." Stone's book is the fruit of that torment. Only when a book is written out of passion is there much hope of its being read with passion. Children, above all, need to feel that they are partners in the quest.

Writing biographies for any age becomes a spiraling process, circling away from oneself, circling back with messages from afar, and all the time circling around one's own autobiography. As long as I can remember, I had wanted to tell my own story directly. Time and again I tried, but I just couldn't find the right voice. I was determined not to write one of those autobiographies that begin with the roster of one's ancestors or a catalogue of one's first memories. I tried to put myself in the third person and to invent a story for myself, but that didn't work either. But when my father died at the age of ninety-six my last link to my childhood was gone, and I felt an urgency to get it all down on paper and make it safe.

It was China, really, that I had wanted to capture — the sights, the sounds, the smells of China. America, too — and me in the midst, feeling all of it. I could see the story line in my own life, and if this had been a biography of someone else I wouldn't have tinkered with the time sequence or with some of the minor facts. But this was *my* story; I could do with it what I pleased. So I labeled the book "fiction," and by tinkering with it and telescoping twelve years into one I felt that I had a more unified book, one that felt more emotionally true to me than if I had carved it up into years. I called the book *Homesick: My Own Story*. I was amazed by how memory hidden for fifty years could turn up as fresh as ever, yet filled with surprises that had never quite surfaced before. And at long last I had a chance to pour out my love for my two countries, China and America.

Actually I had had no idea how deep my loyalty to China ran until my first day in school in America — in eighth grade, in Washington, Pennsylvania, where I was teased about being "the kid from China," I who had thought that once I was in an American school I would feel like a real American. Nor did I realize that the America in which I was taking such joy would be anything but perfect. I went home to my grandmother after that first disillusioning day, spilling over with all the bad news.

The Palmer method of penmanship — that was the worst. The Palmer method, here in the land of the free. My grandmother was working in the garden, and she straightened up with astonishment. "You can only move the underside of your arm when you write?" she asked. "You can't move your fingers at all? They must be preparing you for a crippled old age." Soon we were both laughing. After all, isn't that the only way to face absurdity? And with this shared laughter I was ready to close my story. I had said what I wanted to say, and I ended the book with my grandmother, my grandfather and me walking back to the house, past the cabbages and beans, down the path lined with golden orange chrysanthemums. We stopped to admire the grapes, and I ran ahead to put the plates on the table.

Children with many different kinds of life experiences write to tell me that they identify with this book. Many of them hope that I never gave in to the Palmer method. And I haven't. But one little girl was furious. "You threw me down," she wrote in her letter. "You just stopped your book and never said a word at the end about living happily ever after."

Well, so far, I have been living happily. But having repossessed my childhood, I also needed to go back and see if fifty years later I could also repossess my hometown on the Yangtze River. I was excited at the prospect, but also frightened. What if I felt like a stranger? What if the whole country seemed unfamiliar and I was left an outsider? I hoped to write a book about the experience. In fact, I had already given it a title: *China Homecoming*. But what if I had no story?

The first thing I did on arriving in Hankou was to go to a park beside the Yangtze River and get my fill looking at the river that had run through my dreams for so long. I was sure nothing could change the looks of it, and nothing had. Muddy, mustard-colored and wide, wide, wide — the same as ever. When I turned around, a crowd of people had gathered, as they so often do today around foreigners. I smiled. I was born here, I told them in Chinese, and I spent my childhood here. Now I had come home. And indeed I had; they welcomed me and shook their heads in wonder. Fifty years away and still I had come back. They asked me my age; it's the first question Chinese always ask. A man pointed his chin at my husband, in the way Chinese have. "*Lao tou* — how old is he?" they asked. I burst out laughing. *Lao tou* means "old head" — it's what the Chinese call all white-haired men. I hadn't heard or thought of that expression in all those years, but it had been in my memory all the time, dormant but intact, waiting to be recalled. In that one instant that man returned my childhood to me, whole. So it went. Every day was exciting, full of recoveries and discoveries.

As for my book, I was collecting incidents, people and anecdotes to light up both old China and new. But I wanted my theme to be a personal one. Could I recapture my sense of belonging? There were many moments like the one with the old man on the Yangtze River, but I wanted to build my story to a more climactic scene. And I didn't know how. This is something that you can't research and plan, yet it's one of the ways you write. You take risks, and you wait and see.

I was lucky. Just such a climactic experience occurred toward the end of our stay. I asked our guide if he knew where my little sister had been buried. Yes, he knew; it was now a children's playground. He took us to it. I was delighted to see what a happy place it was today, with children playing all over, on the swings and the jungle gym and in the gazebo. It wasn't until I returned to the hotel that I asked myself whether the guide takes all foreigners there who ask that question, just to make them happy. Was this really the old cemetery?

Of course there was no way to know, but one afternoon my husband and I returned by ourselves to that playground. I didn't know what I was looking for. After all, there had been wars and bombings and revolutions. What could I expect? Nevertheless, I walked slowly around the outer edges of the playground, looking down at the ground all the time. Finally, in a far corner, buried under some brown leaves, I saw a flat broken stone. I leaned over and looked at it, and it had English letters on it: SEARS, it said, and it gave a date of birth and a date of death. It was part of an old gravestone. Obviously this must be the right place. Then I looked at the playground itself, and I noticed that all the benches were of stone, the size of a gravestone. I ran my hand underneath one of those benches, and I could feel the inscription.

By this time, as you can imagine, the Chinese onlookers were extremely curious. What was this foreign woman doing running her hand under their benches? One young woman came over, and I explained to her as well as I could that this had once been a cemetery, and that my sister had been buried here, and that I thought these benches were old gravestones. Immediately she fell in with the idea. She called some young men, and they turned over those benches one by one, and they gathered around, waiting for me to read the inscriptions aloud, telling them the name and nationality of each person: this was a German, born and died in certain years; this was a Russian; this was an American. I never did find my sister's stone, but that no longer mattered to me. I realized that by myself I was uncovering my own small portion of Chinese history. I belonged.

That period of foreign domination was one that the

Chinese preferred to forget. Nevertheless, it was part of their history, I had participated in that time, and now it was my own. It was an experience that I had wanted and that I had been waiting for, without knowing it.

At the end of my visit I knew I still wasn't finished with China; I would be back. With such trips, of course, there are always books involved. When you've been writing as long as I have, your books and your private life mesh; they are of a piece. Time itself ceases to be as linear as it once was. I still eavesdrop as unashamedly as I ever did. I'm still looking for clues.

But I also have a growing suspicion that maybe I did inherit a few hedgehog genes. Not that I have any urge to tie life neatly together in one comprehensive package; I'm not looking for simple explanations. But there are some things I'd like to change. Certainly I would like to see the quality of education in the United States improve. I'd begin by revitalizing the study of history. I talk about this a lot to teachers all over the country. Sometimes I feel uncomfortable while I'm doing it. "What am I doing?" I ask myself. "Am I proselytizing? I should be home writing." But then I realize that I'll never be able to stop trying to convince people how much our future leans on our past. Nor will I be able to stop reaching into the past to enlighten my life today.

JACK PRELUTSKY

In Search of the Addle-pated Paddlepuss

The questions I'm asked most often are: Do I have children? When did I start being a poet? Where do I get my ideas, and how do I write my poems?

I don't have any children. If I did, I don't think I could have ever written my poems, because I love children and I love being around them, and over the past twenty years I've visited thousands of children around the country — none of whose diapers I had to change in the middle of the night. I could store up energy in the middle of the night and get up the next morning and write the poems.

As for when I started being a poet, the truth is I never stopped. A poet is not something you become; a poet is something you are, just as you are a human being. I didn't always know I was a poet. When I was a child I wasn't a particularly good writer. My teachers tended to discourage creativity on my part; they didn't sense any. I flunked English One in college twice and English Two once. Or maybe it was the other way around.

I didn't discover that I could write until I was about twenty-four. I wanted to be an artist, and I used to draw imaginary animals for my own amusement. One evening I sat down and looked at about two dozen of these drawings that had taken me months to draw, and after about two hours I had written two dozen little poems to go with them. I put them aside and didn't think of them for a while. Then a friend saw them and made me take them to his editor. She said, "You are talented." I thought she was going to love my drawings. But she told me I was a terrible artist, and she showed me the work of other illustrators — Arnold Lobel and Maurice Sendak and Tomi Ungerer — and I understood why I was a terrible artist. But she said I had a talent for verse that I didn't suspect I had. As many of the best things are discovered in life, I discovered my gift through serendipity. I was looking for one thing and found something else, but only because I was looking for that first thing.

When I write my poetry for children I have the words in mind, but I also have the child in mind, including the child within myself. I remember that in school I had a librarian who loved books but hated children. We had to go to the library once a week. The first week, when I was in seventh grade, I accidentally discovered a book called *Wild Animals I Have Known* by Ernest Thompson Seton. I had always loved animals — I grew up in the Bronx and spent a lot of time visiting the Bronx Zoo. Well, I hated and feared that librarian so much that I was afraid to go in every week and stand there looking for a book. So I hid *Wild Animals I Have Known* behind some other books. Then, every week, I could just walk into the library, grab the book and sit down with it; I read the same book thirty-six times that year. I had similar feelings about my English teacher; she disliked poetry and was determined to perpetuate her own prejudices in her captives.

Where do my ideas come from? Ideas come from everywhere. They come from everything that has ever happened. They come from everything I have inside. They come from everything I have ever seen or felt or dreamed or read or seen on television or at the movies or remembered or experienced. Things I was told.

One of the main differences between a poet and a non-poet is that a poet knows he is not going to remember what happened. Therefore he is smart enough to carry a notebook and write it down. If I didn't write down what was happening I wouldn't remember it. The brain is a wonderful tool in many ways. But in one way it's like a sieve. If you've ever tried to hold sand in a sieve at the beach, you know you can only hold it for a little while; unless you put a bucket underneath, the sand is gone pretty soon. It's the same thing with an idea — unless you act on an idea, it doesn't stick around very long. I once heard that Albert Einstein was asked why he didn't keep a notebook for his ideas and he said, "Well, I only had one idea."

A poem exists because something happened to a person whom other people choose to call a poet. It exists because something occurred or was felt or dreamed or remembered and the poet chose to communicate it to other people.

Poetry is many things. It's the music of language. It's the stuff that doesn't have to extend to the margin. It's the stuff that can have meter and rhythm. It's the stuff that at its finest says things that prose cannot say. Very often it's something that's comforting to the poet. It's a distillation of experience. But most of all it's communication, right up there with sculpture and photography and painting and music.

One of my earliest poems was a distillation. I looked at a bee one day, and I simply wrote:

> *Every bee*
> *that*
> *ever was*
> *was*
> *partly*
> *sting*
> *and partly*
> *. . . buzz.*

I wrote that twenty-five years ago. Since then I've tried writing other poems about bees and I haven't been able to write a better one. Because, back then, I really didn't know what I was doing.

Another secret of writing, along with taking notes, is keeping your eyes and your ears open, keeping your mind and your heart open, and being aware of what's going on around you. No two poems happen the same way. Writing a poem is like skinning a cat — there's more than one way to do it. To skin a cat it's helpful to have a sharp knife and a steady hand. To write a poem it's useful to have a sharp pencil and a clear head. (Or, again, maybe it's the other way around.) Sometimes I just close my eyes and let the muse take over. Most writers will tell you that often they don't tell the poem or the story what to do; the story or the poem tells them what to do. It takes over. And very often, by the time I've finished a poem it doesn't resemble anything I had set out to create. Never be afraid to let your imagination take wing.

Sometimes I have a rhyme in mind. It can be something as simple as pig/wig. Sometimes it's just a word. A word will come into my mind, like "mucilaginous." (We'll get to that later.) Sometimes it's a couplet. A couplet will just come to me and I'll work in both directions from those two lines. Or it could be a sentence. Or part of a sentence – a beginning with no end, or an end with no beginning; just some vague notion of what I want to say.

When I was a kid I heard poems about hills and daffodils and things like that. The teacher would recite a boring poem:

> Blah, blah, blah, blah, the flower,
> Blah, blah, blah, blah, the tree,

> *Blah, blah, blah, blah, the shower,*
> *Blah, blah, blah, blah, the bee.*

And of course I didn't care much for that. There's a place for that later in life. If I had wanted to hear poems back then — and I wasn't convinced that I did — I probably wanted to hear poems about kids like myself. Or poems about MONSTERS, OUTER SPACE, DRAGONS, DINOSAURS, WEIRD PEOPLE, SPORTS — things that kids can relate to. That's what is wonderful about writers who are writing for children today. They do write about those things.

When I first started compiling anthologies and looking at the writing of other poets I had a lot of trouble with the stuff that was written in the early part of the twentieth century and the latter part of the nineteenth century. It was a Victorian tradition, and it had two unfortunate tendencies. One was a sort of greeting-card verse that was sickeningly sweet and condescending and had no literary merit. The other was poetry that was moralistic and pompous; everything had to have a message, and that was condescending, too. But it doesn't have to be that way. Children aren't stupid. The main differences between children and adults are that children have had fewer experiences — because they haven't been around long enough to have as many as we have had — and they are short. Children love to learn. They learn quickly. So I never condescend when I write for children.

There are different tricks. I have a studio at home that's filled with paraphernalia. Stuff. Like wind-up toys and my miscellaneous frog collection. I put things in my studio because I never know what's going to strike my eye. One day I'll go in there and I'll look at something that I've looked at hundreds of times, and on that day a particular object will say, "Write me today."

I have, for example, a little wind-up mouse that's holding a piece of cheese. You wind it up and it goes *zut zut zut zut* and then it flips over backwards and it goes *zut zut* and it flips over again. About six months after I got the mouse I said, "There's a poem in that mouse," and I wrote a poem called "Boing! Boing! Squeak!"

> Boing! Boing! *Squeak!*
> Boing! Boing! *Squeak!*
> *A bouncing mouse is in my house,*
> *it's been here for a week.*

And I continued from there. I also have a plastic flower "growing" on my window sill, and in my next book there's a poem about growing plastic flowers.

About twenty-five years ago I was in upstate New York and I stopped at a farmhouse. That was something new to me. I hadn't been on farms much; I was born in Brooklyn, grew up in the Bronx and was weaned in Manhattan. I went into a barn and happened to get there when an egg was hatching. It was wonderful. I just sat there for a long time watching the egg crack and watching the little beak come out and the little feathers come out. I was fascinated by it, and I made a few notes. Later I went home and wrote this poem, simply from direct observation. Incidentally, I discovered very early the value of the surprise ending; I may have learned it from O. Henry. Children love to be surprised, so I love to give them little gifts. Often the gift is in the last line of the poem.

THE EGG

If you listen very carefully, you'll hear the chicken
    hatching.
At first there scarcely was a sound, but now a steady
    scratching;
and now the egg begins to crack, the scratching starts to
    quicken,
as anxiously we all await the exit of the chicken.

And now a head emerges from the darkness of the egg,
and now a bit of fluff appears, and now a tiny leg,
and now the chicken's out at last, he's shaking himself
loose.
But, wait a minute, that's no chicken . . . goodness, it's
a goose.

Sometimes I would fall in love, not with the life of the animal, or with the look of the animal, but with the sound of the name of the animal, and I just enjoyed myself. There's something about the word "sneeze," for instance, that has always rung a bell in my head. I've written three or four poems that talk about sneezing: about someone sneezing on a trapeze; about the "sneezy snoozer," someone who sneezes and snoozes at the same time; about a man who sneezes seven times, and each sneeze is louder than the previous one, and on the seventh sneeze his head flies off. Those "eeze" words have always tickled me. Many of my poems were written at the Bronx Zoo, and one day I got to thinking about the weasel — just having fun with the word and seeing what I could do with it. This is what came out:

DON'T EVER SEIZE A WEASEL BY THE TAIL
You should never squeeze a weasel
for you might displease the weasel,
and don't ever seize a weasel by the tail.

[126

Let his tail blow in the breeze;
if you pull it, he will sneeze,
for the weasel's constitution tends to be a little frail.

Yes the weasel wheezes easily;
the weasel freezes easily;
the weasel's tan complexion rather suddenly turns pale.

So don't displease or tease a weasel,
squeeze or freeze or wheeze a weasel
and don't ever seize a weasel by the tail.

Sometimes you take it a step further and you combine the two processes — direct observation and word play. Once I was watching a cow chewing her cud in a field. I liked the idea of a chewing cow, and I also liked the idea of chewing, and I thought, "Well, cows chew. And cows moo." So I just took the thought of what a cow does — it stands there and doesn't do much of anything, it just chews its cud — and those "oo" words started popping into my head. The poem that I wrote was harder than most because I had to combine two different ways of thinking — observation and word play — into one poem, and I came up with this:

THE COW
The cow mainly moos as she chooses to moo
and she chooses to moo as she chooses.

She furthermore chews as she chooses to chew
and she chooses to chew as she muses.

If she chooses to moo she may moo to amuse
or may moo just to moo as she chooses.

If she chooses to chew she may moo as she chews
or may chew just to chew as she muses.

One of my first jobs when I got out of high school was working at a commercial factor company in midtown Manhattan. I wasn't cut out for it. My co-workers had several nicknames for me, and one of them was "the Snail." I was called the Snail because I tended to do things at my own pace. It was a very different pace from the one that the people who were running the company wanted to pay me for. After they relieved me of my duties, permanently, I thought about that. As it happens, over the years I've written many autobiographical poems that I've disguised as animal poems. When I was younger, for example, I was a very insular person; it was hard to get to know me. So I wrote of myself as a turtle hiding inside a shell. This time I wrote of myself as a snail:

> *The snail doesn't know where he's going*
> *and he doesn't especially care,*

one place is as good as another
and here is no better than there.

The snail's unconcerned with direction
but happily goes on his way
in search of specifically nothing
at two or three inches a day.

As I began to learn more about writing and about children I increasingly started to write from my own childhood experiences, drawing on things that really happened. Something wonderful occurs when you do that. The more you do it, the easier it gets; the more you write down what happened to you when you were a child, the more you will remember.

I had a childhood friend named Willie, and one day, when the rest of us were hanging around — Harvey, Lumpy, Tony and I — he came out into the street and said, "Look at that!" We said, "What?" He said, "There's a worm on the sidewalk." We had all seen worms before, and we didn't think much about it one way or the other. But then he said, "You know, that looks *good!*" And he ate it. Willie and I had an agreement that if one of us did something new, the other one had to do it — right then and there. When Willie did things, by the way, he did them right. He didn't just eat some little pinkie-size worm, because anybody can eat those. He ate

129]

one of those big, long, fat, red, juicy worms.

This happened when I was about eight years old. I had completely forgotten it until I was in my thirties and began writing about some of the things that happened to me when I was a kid in the Bronx. And one of the things I suddenly remembered was that I had eaten a worm. So I wrote the following poem. It's direct experience, that's all it is. I wrote it the way it happened.

WILLIE ATE A WORM

Willie ate a worm today,
a squiggly, wiggly worm.
He picked it up
from the dust and dirt
and wiped it off
on his brand-new shirt.
Then slurp, slupp
he ate it up,
yes Willie ate a worm today,
a squiggly, wiggly worm.

Willie ate a worm today,
he didn't bother to chew,
and we all stared
and we all squirmed
when Willie swallowed
down that worm.

> *Then slupp, slurp*
> *Willie burped,*
> *yes Willie ate a worm today,*
> *I think I'll eat one too.*

I remember one period of several years when I was having a lot of trouble writing. Nothing was coming out — real writer's block. I didn't know what to do. So I started asking teachers and librarians, "What should I write about? What do kids want to hear about?" And they all told me the same thing: monsters. (Today they will tell you dinosaurs.) I suddenly remembered that when I was a kid my mother used to threaten me, her own son, with the bogeyman. Her method was simple:

"Mommy, I don't want to eat my spinach."

"You eat your spinach or the bogeyman is going to get you!"

"O.K., I'll eat my spinach."

"Mommy, I don't want to go to bed."

"You go to bed or the bogeyman is going to get you."

"All right, I'll go to bed."

He never got me, by the way. I figured out that the reason he didn't get me was not because my mother was lying to me, but because we lived in a bad neighborhood. He would rather stay in his own domicile and wait for me to come to him.

Well, I wrote a poem about the bogeyman and later I started reading books of folklore, particularly about the traditional scary creatures of popular culture — werewolves, zombies, witches . . . But the bogeyman has always interested me the most because he was the one my mother used on me. I wrote this poem in the middle of the night. (I wrote all the poems in *Nightmares* between midnight and six in the morning; I couldn't seem to write them at any other time.) What I did was to draw a word picture of what I thought the bogeyman should be and what I thought my mother had in mind when she was saying these terrible things to her gullible little boy.

THE BOGEYMAN

In the desolate depths of a perilous place
the bogeyman lurks, with a snarl on his face.
Never dare, never dare to approach his dark lair
for he's waiting . . . just waiting . . . to get you.

He skulks in the shadows, relentless and wild
in his search for a tender, delectable child.
With his steely sharp claws and his slavering jaws
oh he's waiting . . . just waiting . . . to get you.

[132

Many have entered his dreary domain
but not even one has been heard from again.
They no doubt made a feast for the butchering beast
and he's waiting . . . just waiting . . . to get you.

In that sulphurous, sunless and sinister place
he'll crumple your bones in his bogey embrace.
Never never go near if you hold your life dear,
for oh! . . . what he'll do . . . when he gets you!

In other words, I took my mother's monster threat
and turned it into a poem. Over the years I've learned
that every experience should be treated as an oppor-
tunity for creativity, whether it's a good experience
or a bad one or an indifferent one. For instance, I like
to do a little woodworking around the house, and one
day six or seven years ago I was building some shelves.
We had recently moved into a house, and I was building a large cabinet. I built it in one piece. It turned out
to be too big to fit through a door or to move from
my shop, so I built it on-site, in the living room, on
the wall-to-wall carpet. I was gluing it up, and I had
spread newspapers everywhere. But Murphy's Law,
which says that if something can go wrong it will, is a
wonderful law; it's a law that's rarely broken. Well,
the phone rings and I run to get it. I'm barefoot. I stub
my toe on the edge of a board and continue running

to the phone. I'm talking on the phone and I'm looking back in horror, because I realize that what I've
also done is to tip over a quart of woodworker's glue,
which has found its way through the one gap in the
newspapers in the entire room and is seeping into the
carpet.

The carpet was irreclaimable — we had to rip the
whole thing up. I didn't like it anyway. But at the
time we couldn't afford to replace it. I looked at that
glue oozing over the carpet and I started to anthropomorphize the glue. That's a wonderful technique,
by the way; you can anthropomorphize anything —
make it come alive. And that's what I did. I created
glue creatures that I called gloppers. At first I had
them as "gloppy gloopers," but that didn't work out
for purposes of rhyme. Finally I turned them into
"gloopy gloppers," and I created these mucilaginous —
I told you we'd get back to that word — gelatinous
gloopy gloppers, as follows:

SONG OF THE GLOOPY GLOPPERS

We are Gloppers, gloopy Gloppers,
mucilaginous, gelatinous,
we never fail to find a frail
yet filling form to fatten us,
we ooze about the countryside,
through hamlet and metropolis,

for Gloppers ooze where Gloppers choose,
enveloping the populace.

We are Gloppers, gloopy Gloppers,
unrelenting, irresistible,
what we will do to you is too
distressing to be listable,
we'll ooze into your living room,
your kitchen, and your vestibule,
and in your bed we'll taste your head,
to test if you're digestible.

We are Gloppers, gloopy Gloppers,
globs of undulating Glopper ooze,
you cannot quell our viscid swell,
there is no way to stop our ooze,
for Gloppers are invincible,
unquenchable, unstoppable,
and when we swarm upon your form,
we know we'll find you GLOPPABLE!

Sometimes a writer is faced with an interesting problem: you have to write about something you know nothing about. Writers do this all the time — open almost any magazine and you'll see. In my most recent book, a small book of dinosaur poems called *Tyrannosaurus Was a Beast*, I had the problem of wanting a magnificent huge dinosaur to end the book with. I was stuck. But sometimes blessings happen.

The very week that I needed a dinosaur, a new one was discovered. Not only that; it was discovered a few miles from my house, right outside the city of Albuquerque, and it was the largest land creature ever on earth. The story was on the front page of the newspaper. It was one of the psauropods, called seismosaurus, which means "earth shaker," and I knew nothing about it. All I knew about seismosaurus was that I wanted to end the book with it and that it was big. I opened *Roget's Thesaurus*, my favorite reference book, to the word "big," and this is what I wrote:

SEISMOSAURUS

Seismosaurus was enormous,
Seismosaurus was tremendous,
Seismosaurus was prodigious,
Seismosaurus was stupendous.

Seismosaurus was titanic,
Seismosaurus was colossal,
Seismosaurus now is nothing
but a monumental fossil.

All those big words, by the way, are in the exact order that they appear in the thesaurus. You can check it.

Usually we're unaware that we are storing up images. Then one day, suddenly, a lot of things just come together. When I was a kid there was a television program called "You Asked for It." One of the things I saw on that show was a cat that played ping-pong. There was a man at one end of the table hitting the ball, and at the other end was a cat. The cat never missed. A few years ago I went to the University of Oregon, in Eugene, to give a talk, and they put me up with a local couple. The man's two interests seemed to be astronomy and ping-pong. He had a ping-pong table in the basement. We played, and he beat me 21–0. Then he said, "Now I'll play just half of your side of the table and I'll hit all my shots to either your forehand or your backhand — you choose which." And he beat me 21–3. Then he did the same using half the table and playing with his wallet and spotting me 16 points, and he still beat me easily.

Well, "You Asked for It" and the ping-pong-playing cat and this fellow in the basement in Eugene all came together, and I wrote the following poem, which is from a book called *Something Big Has Been Here*, a sequel to *The New Kid on the Block*.

THE ADDLE-PATED PADDLEPUSS

The Addle-pated Paddlepuss
is agile as a cat,
its neck is long and limber,

and its face is broad and flat,
it moves with skill and vigor,
with velocity and grace,
as it spends its every second
playing ping-pong with its face.

The Addle-pated Paddlepuss
prevails in every game,
its opponent doesn't matter,
the result is all the same,
with its supersonic smashes
and its convoluted spins,
it demolishes all comers
and invariably wins.

The Addle-pated Paddlepuss,
with effervescent verve,
follows innovative volleys
with a scintillating serve,
if you're fond of playing ping-pong
and would like to lose in style,
the Addle-pated Paddlepuss
will serve you for awhile.

KATHERINE PATERSON

Heart in Hiding

I was twenty years old. I remember how hot the room seemed, though it was January. It was the first day in a course called "Nineteenth Century English Literature." In the fall semester I had studied Milton and Donne and was sure that nothing of any worth had happened in English lit since the close of the seventeenth century. "Nineteenth Century" was a seminar course, and each of us was to do a paper. When my turn came to say what writer I would select, I racked my brain for anyone who might have been born English in that boring century and finally said "Kipling," having been read *Just So Stories* on my mother's lap.

"Katherine," I heard Dr. Winship saying, "you

don't want to write on Kipling. You want to write on Gerard Manley Hopkins."

How could I want to write on Gerard Manley Hopkins? It was the first time I had ever heard the name. But Dr. Winship said I wanted to write about this person, and I had learned that Dr. Winship generally knew what he was talking about. So that afternoon I went to the library to meet the object of this arranged marriage. I remember all too well the first poem I read. It was "The Windhover."

I caught this morning's minion, kingdom of daylight's
    dauphin, dapple-dawn-drawn Falcon, in his riding
Of the rolling level underneath him steady air, and
    striding
High there, how he rung upon the rein of a wimpling
    wing
In his ecstacy! . . .

I would like to tell you tonight that my first encounter with Gerard Manley Hopkins filled me with ecstasy. Actually it was more like panic. If you've read my book *The Great Gilly Hopkins* you'll remember the scene where Gilly, who thinks of herself as a terrific reader, arrogantly opens *The Oxford Book of English Verse* to read aloud to the old man who lives next door and stumbles into:

[142

Sumer is icumen in,
Lhude sing cuccu!
Groweth sed, and bloweth med,
And springth the wude nu —
Sing cuccu!

Cuckoo was right. "Wait a minute," [Gilly] muttered, turning the page.

bytuene Mershe ant Averil . . .

She looked quickly at the next.

Lenten ys come with love to toune, . . .

And the next —

Ichot a burde in boure bryht,
That fully semly is on syht, . . .

She slammed the book shut. They were obviously trying to play a trick on her. Make her seem stupid. See, there was Mr. Randolph giggling to himself. "It's not in English!" she yelled. "You're just trying to make a fool of me."

"The Windhover" didn't seem to be in any English that I knew. But I also knew that Dr. Winship was not trying to make a fool out of me; he wasn't that kind of professor. He had said that I would want to do Hopkins. He not only thought I should be able to understand this mad poet; he thought I would like him. So, by golly, I would find out why or die in the attempt.

The first thing I did was get a dictionary and look up the meaning of every word in the poem that I was fuzzy on, beginning with "windhover." When I had in mind the literal meaning of every word, I began to read the poem over and over again. At last, in desperation, I read it aloud. The rest, as they say, is history. I went on to write the paper. The next year I did my undergraduate thesis on Hopkins, and through the thirty-six years since that January morning I've gone back again and again to my slender volume of Hopkins's poetry for inspiration, for nourishment and for comfort.

Gilly Hopkins is, of course, Gerard Manley's namesake, though I wasn't aware of the relationship at first. I think of my first reading of "The Windhover" whenever a teacher, a parent or a librarian begins to talk about allowing children to make their own reading choices. I believe in freedom of choice as much as anyone. But the young don't know the rich variety of choices that are available. Someone they trust must be wise and bold enough to hand them something they would never have known to choose. I remember the day I met Gerard Manley Hopkins as a pivotal moment in my life. It would be years before I would think of myself as a writer, and I've never thought of myself as a poet. But something happened to me that day I find hard to articulate. I learned something about how language works on the ear and the mind and the heart.

Kokoro is the Japanese word for heart. But it's not simply heart as the seat of the emotions; *kokoro* is also the seat of the intellect — the mind/heart, if you will. Thus the Sino-Japanese character for "idea" combines the ideograph for the word "sound" with the ideograph for *kokoro*. So an idea is a sound from the heart. If you want to write the character that means "to imagine," you make the ideograph for "tree." Then you put an eye spying out from behind the tree. Then, below the eye spying out from behind the tree, you again put *kokoro*, or heart. Which is why I named a book about reading and writing children's books *The Spying Heart*.

All of this is to explain what happened to me when I began reading Gerard Manley Hopkins. As I read "The Windhover" aloud, something happened in my mind/heart, my *kokoro*, that I truly understood but that I was incapable of articulating. In "The Windhover," Hopkins says:

. . . My heart in hiding
Stirred for a bird, — the achieve of, the mastery of the
  thing!

My heart in hiding stirred when I was reading Hopkins in a way it had almost never stirred except when I heard certain passages in the King James Bible.

Many years later another poem by Hopkins, "Spring and Fall: To a Young Child," explained to me what writing for children was all about.

> *Márgarét, are you grieving*
> *Over Goldengrove unleaving?*
> *Leáves, líke the things of man, you*
> *With your fresh thoughts care for, can you?*
> *Áh! ás the heart grows older*
> *It will come to such sights colder*
> *By and by, nor spare a sigh*
> *Though worlds of wanwood leafmeal lie;*
> *And yet you will weep and know why.*
> *Now no matter, child, the name:*
> *Sórrow's springs áre the same.*
> *Nor mouth had, no nor mind, expressed*
> *What heart heard of, ghost guessed:*
> *It ís the blight man was born for,*
> *It is Margaret you mourn for.*

What I think I'm doing when I write for the young is to articulate the glorious but fragile human condi-

[146

tion for those whose hearts have heard but whose mouths, at the age of five or ten or fourteen, can't yet express. But the truth is that I can't really express it either. So what happens is a reciprocal gift between writer and reader: one heart in hiding reaching out to another. We are trying to communicate that which lies in our deepest heart, which has no words, which can only be hinted at through the means of a story. And somehow, miraculously, a story that comes from deep in my heart calls from a reader that which is deepest in his or her heart, and together from our secret hidden selves we create a story that neither of us could have told alone.

When we think of the world of childhood, our first thought is how exposed it is. Children are constantly being stripped and bathed, commanded to eat when they aren't hungry, asked about their most private feelings or told they shouldn't feel the way they do. They are kissed and squeezed by strangers who claim some mysterious right of kinship or friendship. They hear themselves and their bloodlines discussed as if they were livestock in an agricultural show. And I'm only talking about children who are loved and cared for. The exposure of the despised or neglected child is too painful to imagine.

As adults we often assume that we have the authority to tell our children what to do and what to be and how to feel. How dare we? It follows, therefore, that parents and teachers think that people who write books for children ought to be on the adults' side. The question I get most often from people who know I write for children but who have never read my books is: What message are you trying to teach children through your books? Or, if they're a bit more sophisticated: What moral values do your books impart to young readers? I try not to get testy. After all, I don't like it when people who *have* read my books complain that I'm corrupting the morals of the young or, conversely, when critics say that my books are too didactic and moralistic. What I think I'm doing when I write a book for the young is to connect with the part of the child that's hidden. I'm trying to write a story.

Last spring I watched an educational television program called "In Search of the Mind." Everybody, it seems, knows what a brain is, but nobody quite knows what a mind is. "The mind is what the brain does," the narrator said, conceding that he had solved none of the mysteries of the mind with that sentence. To me the most moving episode dealt with the British musician Clive Wearing. A few years ago this gifted young artist and conductor was struck by a strange inflammation of his brain that virtually destroyed his memory. "It's as though he's wearing blinkers," his wife said. "Every moment is separated in time from every other moment." Every moment is an awakening into consciousness. Wearing can't make the connections that every child takes for granted. The imaging of the past and the future with which each one of us composes the narratives of our lives is not possible for him. He writes constantly in his diary, trying to preserve a fleeting moment. But the next moment he will wonder how those words got on that page, or indeed where the diary itself came from.

Otherwise his intellect is not impaired, which makes his condition even more tragic, and he is often deeply depressed. Yet there are two elements of his former, rich life that haven't deserted him. The first is his love for his wife. Every time he sees her, which may be five minutes since he last saw her, he throws his arms around her and greets her with great joy, welcoming her back into his life as though she had been gone for years. In his diary he writes on almost every page, "I love Debby for ever and ever" — even though for Clive Wearing there is no "ever."

The second element of his past life that mysteriously remains is music. On the TV program, we watch as his wife takes him into a room where there is a piano and a small group of singers. At first he seems confused; he says he doesn't know how to play. But his wife gently urges him to try. He strikes a few chords, the singers start to sing, and immediately the face of Clive Wearing is transformed as he sings and conducts Mozart's "Ave Verum Corpus." Somehow love and music have remained whole in his ravaged brain. No one can explain why this can be, when the rest of his memory seems to have been destroyed. But somehow in his mind and heart — his *kokoro* — there is this miraculous survival of love and beauty.

I like to think that when we write for children we are working with the basic stuff of life. Taking a clue from Clive Wearing, I'd suggest that the basic stuff of life is love and beauty. In this argument I have on my side, surprisingly, the evidence of modern science. Unlike the scientific materialism of a past generation, modern neuroscience believes in what we call mind: a human intellect and will, a *kokoro* that can't be reduced to brain matter. In fact, modern physics contends that the universe posits mind — intellect and will — that can't be reduced to the elements of matter. Physicists have theorized, and observation seems to bear out, that matter is finite, that the universe had a beginning, has a middle and will have an end. But around and beyond the finite universe, as a growing number of scientists affirm, there is an eternal intellect and will — a mind that existed before the Big Bang, a mind that created all matter out of nothing.

Some of the scientists have been driven to this conclusion by their observation of how the universe seems to work. The first question that today's physicists ask of a new theory is: "Is it beautiful?" For experience has taught them that truth is invariably beautiful. Nor do they think that this beauty can be reduced to either chance or necessity. As the physicist Henry Margenau explains, "We do not believe that beauty is only in the eye of the beholder. There are objective features underlying at least some experiences of beauty, such as the frequency ratios of the notes of a major chord, symmetry of geometric forms, or the aesthetic appeal of juxtaposed complementary colors. None of these has survival value, but all are prevalent in nature in a measure hardly compatible with chance. We marvel at the song of the birds, the color scheme of flowers (do insects have a sense of aesthetics?), of birds' feathers, and at the incomparable beauty of a fallen maple leaf, its deep red coloring, its blue veins and its golden edges. Are these qualities useful for survival when the leaf is about to decay?" James Watson, in his book about the discovery of the double-helix structure of DNA, says, "So we had lunch, telling each other that a structure this pretty just had to exist."

What are the properties of beauty to a physicist? There are three: simplicity, harmony and brilliance. Most discussions of physics mystify me. But beauty is a quality I know something about. A few summers ago I was lying on the couch at our summer house reading a new book. When I finished I said to my husband, "This is a beautiful book."

"What's it about?" he asked.

Instead of answering, I burst into tears. I was amazed at the power of my reaction, but those of you who have read *Sarah, Plain and Tall,* by Patricia Mac-Lachlan, will understand. It *is* a beautiful book, and tears are an appropriate response to beauty.

But for a moment let's apply the scientist's test of beauty. Simplicity? Yes, the book is complete in it-self — direct and without superfluous words. Harmony? You'd have to look far to find a book in which the parts — character, setting and plot — so gracefully conform to one another and to the language of the whole. Brilliance? Here, like the scientist, we aren't talking about intellectual cleverness but about clarity — about the light that the book sheds not only on itself but beyond itself, to other stories and other lives.

Don't you keep thinking of it? Don't you compare other books to it? Don't you know the prairie better now? And what it means to care about another person?

Beauty, so defined, is a good test to apply to art of any kind — perhaps particularly to the art of children's books. For the stories that have endured, the stories to which we turn as we seek to shape our lives, are all beautiful in this sense.

The stories that have shaped me most are the stories of the Bible. I know this is true, but I often try to figure out *how* those stories have shaped me. How has the Bible made me the writer I am?

For most of us the image of history or of chronological time is a line. Whenever I see a straight line drawn on a piece of paper or on a blackboard I will, in my head, draw a perpendicular line at either end. In my mind and my psyche, time has both a beginning and an end. At the beginning of the line I mentally write CREATION and at the end write ESCHATON, the end of history. Surrounding this bounded finite line is the great expanse of unmarked paper or blackboard representing unmarked, unbounded eternity. But there is another perpendicular line that bisects my finite line. It's there somewhere between the beginning and the end, always much nearer the right-hand end of the line than the left. This line differs from the other two because it's in the form of a cross.

If you grew up in the religious tradition that I did, after you have located those three basic marks on the line, you add others. One, toward the beginning, is labeled "the call of Abraham." Another is labeled "the exodus," another "the reign of David," another "the fall of Jerusalem." Sometimes I affix approximate historical dates to these intermediate marks. Once I drew one of these familiar lines and put a tiny mark far to the right and labeled it "ME 1932" — thereby rather grandly putting myself into sacred history. But it's only grandiose, really, if, when I put my own name in, I exclude anyone else's. Because the Bible affirms that all God's creatures have a place of significance in sacred history. Jesus said, "Are not five sparrows sold for two farthings, and not one of them is forgotten before God? But even the very hairs of your head are all numbered. Fear not therefore: ye are of more value than many sparrows." The words sound to me like those of a mother, gently teasing her much-beloved child who has come to her crushed and full of self-doubt.

But back to the time line. What those three primary marks and the secondary marks on the line say to me is something that I find remarkably echoed in my reading of modern physics, which is that time is finite. Within the infinite expanse of eternity, time as we know it on our small planet moves purposefully from beginning to end. Beyond this exciting hypothesis I also see in the Bible the affirmation that, at certain critical points in human history, time is invaded in a special way by the eternal.

By now you've caught on that my view of time is not really Einstein's view, or Newton's, or even the view that most of us have when we set our alarm clocks or consult our daily calendar. My view of time has been shaped by a distinctly biblical view, which is largely ignorant of most scientific or philosophical arguments about the nature of time but which is still a very helpful model for someone who wants to write fiction.

Eudora Welty once said that "Southerners do have, they've inherited, a narrative sense of human destiny." And this "narrative sense of human destiny" is closely related to that time line on the blackboard. Of course that's why the South is known as the Bible Belt. We in the South were raised on this book that has a beginning, a middle and an end — a coherent plot, with wonderful, richly human characters, a vivid setting and a powerful theme.

I want to address the question of theme in the biblical narrative, because it's not a matter that everyone who reads the Bible would agree on. Some people see the theme of the Bible in terms of morality. They maintain that there is a moral law woven into the fabric of the universe, a basic difference between right and wrong. People who do right, though they may suffer along the way, will eventually be rewarded, and those who do wrong, though they seem temporarily to prosper, will ultimately be punished.

I'm not going to get myself in trouble here by telling you that there's no difference between right and wrong and that a person who sows rutabagas will end up picking roses. I believe there *is* a difference between right and wrong, and observation teaches me that in the long run people and societies seem to reap what they sow. But I don't think morality is the basic theme of the Bible. I think its theme is closer to what physicists would call beauty. By itself, morality is not beautiful enough. Listen to Genesis: "And God said, Let there be light: and there was light. And God saw the light, that it was good: . . . And God saw every thing that he had made, and, behold, it was very good." The word "good" is not a moral judgment but an aesthetic one. God saw that what He had made was very beautiful.

Another passage, this one from the Gospels: "And suddenly there was with the angel a multitude of the heavenly host praising God, and saying, Glory to God in the highest, and on earth peace, good will toward men."

I can't hear those words without hearing the Gloria in Mozart's Twelfth Mass, speaking of beauty. The beauty of those words tells me what the Bible is all about. The Bible does mention eternity, but only as background for the real drama, which is a story of Earth, or, even more narrowly, a story of humanity's brief appearance on Earth. This is also the stuff of fiction — the actions of human beings within the limits of time and space. But the Bible says something more: that the posture of the eternal Creator toward the finite creation is that of good will. Listen, once more, to Gerard Manley Hopkins:

The world is charged with the grandeur of God.
*   It will flame out, like shining from shook foil;*
*   It gathers to a greatness, like the ooze of oil*
Crushed. Why do men then now not reck his rod?
Generations have trod, have trod, have trod;
*   And all is seared with trade; bleared, smeared with toil;*
*   And wears man's smudge and shares man's smell: the*
*   soil*
Is bare now, nor can foot feel, being shod.

And for all this, nature is never spent;
  There lives the dearest freshness deep down things;
And though the last lights off the black West went
  Oh, morning, at the brown brink eastward, springs —
Because the Holy Ghost over the bent
  World broods with warm breast and with ah! bright
  wings.

Every society, as Joseph Campbell has demonstrated, has its myths by which it finds meaning for life, and those myths have certain similarities. For example, the story of the hero who sets out into a realm of supernatural wonder, meets and conquers fabulous foes and returns again to bestow boons on his fellows — this is a story that occurs over and over in the mythologies and folk and fairy tales of the world. But even as I consider the paradigm of the universal story of the hero, I flesh it out with Abraham and Jacob and Moses and Jesus and see evidence throughout of the good will of the Creator toward creation — the Holy Ghost brooding like a mother bird on her nest over the bent world. It's not that I don't know other stories; it's just that Bible stories have had the most influence over me.

That's why I become uncomfortable when people ask me about the morals of my stories or the values

I'm trying to impart. Moral judgment is not my prerogative. Of course, I'll make moral judgments for myself, and as a parent I'll try to teach my children what I believe to be right and good and what I see as evil and wrong. I'll also do whatever I can to work for peace and justice, which I believe to be good and right, and to combat war and oppression, which I believe to be evil. But when it comes to passing judgment on other people, even my own children, I have to tread carefully. Moral judgment is the prerogative of the Creator, and if the Bible is to be believed, when the Creator makes a moral judgment it breaks His heart.

So when I write a story for children it's not to make moral judgments, though the story may portray the observed human truth that behavior has consequences. I'm seeking to tell a story from my heart — my *kokoro* — with the hope that it will speak to another heart. I'll try to make the story as good as I can — good in the sense of beautiful. And, again, I define that beauty by the qualities of simplicity, harmony and brilliance.

Simplicity. This is the quality I have the least trouble with. E. B. White said somewhere that he thought he was ideally suited to writing for children because he didn't have a very big vocabulary. I think we'd all agree that Mr. White had a vocabulary equal to whatever need arose. But I understand what he was saying. I think I'm ideally suited to writing for children because I have a simple mind. I don't catch on to things quickly; I have to struggle with questions the way a dog worries a bone. I prefer the concrete to the abstract. I'm forever trying to reduce everything troublesome or mysterious to a story, or at least to a simile or a metaphor. So, for example, when my eight-year-old son's best friend is killed during the same period when I must struggle with the fact that I've had cancer and am frighteningly mortal, I don't turn to philosophy or theology; I write a story. By writing fiction, which must have a beginning, a middle and an end, I give shape to what seems chaotic and unmanageable in my life. Writing stories is much cheaper than psychotherapy — and far more satisfying.

Harmony is a quality I have more trouble with, certainly if you listen to some of my critics. A book of mine that has garnered considerable abuse is *Jacob Have I Loved*, which many critics felt was out of balance, out of harmony. I often don't know what I'm doing when I write, but in the case of the ending of *Jacob* I was wide awake. I made a deliberate decision to compress Louise's college years to a very few pages, and I jumped from Rass Island to Truitt Valley, with hardly a steppingstone in between, because I wasn't interested in the academic curriculum of either the University of Maryland or the University of Kentucky. It seemed to me that Louise's higher education had very little to do with what Jill Paton Walsh calls the "trajectory" of the story. In her essay "The Lords of Time," she says: "The trajectory of a book is the route chosen by the author through his material. It is the action of a book, considered not as the movement of paraphrasable events in that book but as the movement of the author's exposition and the reader's experience of it. And a good trajectory is the optimum, the most emotionally loaded flight path across the subject to the projected end."

Every book has its unique trajectory, although the genre will lead you to expect a certain kind. If you're reading a love story, as Jill Paton Walsh says, and the hero is about to kiss the heroine, you become annoyed if the author suddenly decides to insert a police chase. Whereas if you're reading what's meant to be a detective story and the author freezes the chase and pans to a tender love scene just when the murderer is about to be apprehended, you may well skip the romantic scene to get on with the chase. Readers do tend to sense what does or doesn't belong on the trajectory of a particular story. Some years ago I was reading a powerful novel and in the middle of it the writer supplied the recipe for a favorite food. It was a good recipe; I may have even made it for my own family. But as a reader I was jarred.

I used to think that children hated descriptions. But they only hate descriptions that are stuck in for effect, that don't belong on the trajectory. You could no more have *The Secret Garden* without lengthy descriptions of the garden than you could have *Charlotte's Web* without paying tribute to the changing seasons. Though neither element actually furthers the plot, both of them are on the trajectory. They are vital to the harmony of the book.

When you think of harmony you have to consider every element that has gone into a book. When I was writing *Jacob* I tried to write it in third person, simply because I don't like writing in first person; it seems to me an arrogant and limiting point of view. But I found to my unhappiness that the book was refusing to be told in any voice but Louise's. Now, many years later, I can say, "Well, of course. How obvious. Jealousy can only speak in the first person. It can't imagine another point of view." To maintain the harmony of the book, the point of view had to be first person singular. Think about the play *Amadeus*. A great deal of its power derives from the voice of Salieri telling the tale.

Finally, brilliance. I once said to my editor, Virginia Buckley, when we were struggling with a passage in one of my books, that a suggestion by the copy editor would ruin the rhythm of a particular sentence. "Rhythm," I intoned solemnly, "is everything." Then I heard myself add, "But clarity is more." I rewrote the passage.

I often think of the time I wrote a speech when *The Master Puppeteer* won the National Book Award. I had to write in one afternoon what became known in the family as "Mother's 500 Deathless Words" and dictate them on the telephone to Virginia that evening. This was to be my first real venture in the public eye as a writer, and I was to share the stage with, among others, Richard Eberhardt, Erskine Caldwell, Bruno Bettelheim, Irving Howe, Jacques Barzun and C. P. Snow. To say the least, I was a little nervous.

My children couldn't imagine why it would take anyone eight hours to write 500 words, but when Virginia called I had to stop frantically revising; my time had run out. As nervous as I was about the 500 words, I thought I had a sockeroo ending. And with a sockeroo ending, who would worry about the other 495? At Virginia's suggestion I read the whole speech through and then went back and read it sentence by sentence so that she could take it down. When I got to my sockeroo five-word final sentence the second time, there was a long pause at the other end of the line. Finally a gentle voice said, "It sounds wonderful, Katherine, but what does it *mean?*" Now, whenever I'm revising and I come upon a particularly felicitous group of words, I apply the "sounds wonderful, but what does it mean?" test.

Perhaps the basic test for beauty in a book — simplicity, harmony and brilliance (or clarity) — is to read the whole story aloud, preferably at one sitting. In fact, I don't think this is a test only for children's books; I'm suspicious of any book that can't be read aloud. But for a children's writer there is hardly any exercise more helpful. I was very troubled about *Park's Quest* until, by chance, I was asked to read it aloud to a blind friend, and when it worked out loud I knew it was all right. It would do.

The problem with the book, though, was that it was in the shadow of the powerful legend of Parsifal, and I could only compare my feeble words on the page with that immortal story. Usually the specific myth or legend or folktale behind a book is more or less subconscious. I certainly didn't know — as someone later explained to me — that *Gilly Hopkins* was a retelling of *Pilgrim's Progress;* I had thought it was the Prodigal Son. But with *Park's Quest* I knew from the beginning, even before I knew where the story would be set or who its characters would be, that its

[164

overriding shape would be that of the Parsifal legend as retold by the German romantic poet Wolfram in the early thirteenth century.

This was the only time I've seen quite so clearly the legend behind the story I was trying to tell. Certainly the story of Jacob and Esau is background to *Jacob Have I Loved*, but in a less direct way. But now, after nine novels, I can see that the overarching theme of them all is the biblical theme of divine good will. The more common word for good will in the Old Testament is loving-kindness. In the New Testament it's called grace. Like God, good will can't be defined. We are always reduced to simile, to metaphor, to once-upon-a-time.

I fell in love with the story of Parsifal before I had ever really heard it, before I knew what a powerful story of good will it was. I fell in love with it when I heard a speaker at the National Women's Conference to Prevent Nuclear War say: "We cannot frighten people into responsibility. People are so frightened now that they have to deny that there is a nuclear threat. I think what we must do is ask the question of Parsifal."

A shiver went through my body. I didn't know what the question of Parsifal was. But I knew I had to find out.

In the legend as Wolfram tells it, Parsifal, the Grail

Knight, is brought by enchantment to the castle of the Grail King. The king is suffering from a wound that will not heal, and he will only be healed on the day the Grail Knight appears and asks the question. The young Parsifal, however, is the prototype of the innocent fool. He has no idea that he is the Grail Knight. When he finds himself in the mysterious castle of the Grail he's not about to ask any questions, because he has been told by those wiser than he that a man who keeps asking questions appears to be even more of a fool than he is.

So he doesn't ask the question. The king is not healed. And Parsifal is thrown out of the castle on his ear. In his subsequent wanderings our innocent fool becomes sadder and, if not wiser, certainly less gullible and increasingly world-weary. Try as he will, he can't find his way back to the Grail Castle. He refuses to return to Camelot, convinced that he is no longer worthy to take his seat at the Round Table. Eventually he loses all track of space and time until finally he loses his faith as well.

Then one day in the forest he comes upon a family of pilgrims. They are amazed to see a knight armed and in armor, for it is Good Friday. They speak to the despairing Parsifal, and he takes heart. Perhaps, he thinks, the One mighty enough to bring the world into being would have the power to bring comfort to his lost and despairing soul. Parsifal seeks out a hermit, who tells him again the gospel story, hears his confession and sends him once more on his quest. At last Parsifal comes a second time to the Grail Castle, and this time he asks the suffering king the question. "Dear Uncle," Parsifal asks, "what aileth thee?" Upon hearing these compassionate words the king is healed. And so is Parsifal himself.

In my book *Park's Quest*, Parkington Waddell Broughton V is also the innocent fool, unaware that he is the Grail Knight entrusted with the compassionate question, and so he fails his quest and loses his way in the wilderness. Now, as I've explained, I believe that there is an eternal mind who created from nothing a universe of beauty and whose posture toward all is that of loving-kindness, grace, good will. Thus you will suspect that in the world as I know it — and therefore in all my books — even in the darkest wilderness, there are angels, and a knight, no matter how lost and despairing, will always be given another chance to fulfill his quest. This is the final passage from *Park's Quest*:

With Park easing the wheels down over the stoop and Thanh holding on to the footrests, they were able to get the chair off the porch with only a minor jolt.

"Okay?" Thanh asked the old man.

Park turned the chair around and started slowly toward the gate. Once out of the yard, Thanh tried once more to take over the pushing.

"He like fast," she said. "Don't you like fast?"

"No," Park said. "Not tonight. It's dark. We gotta see where we're going."

"Yellow chicken," she said amicably, shrugging an apology to the old man, and then, with Jupe frolicking around her legs, she danced ahead of them down the road. As the path dropped off more steeply, Park had to hold back to keep the chair from racing downhill. In the moonlight he felt as though he were following fairy shadows. He wondered if the old man sensed the enchantment.

By the time they got to the gate, she was standing there, holding it open. "What I do," she said. "I go get water. Take to crow. Get gun. You wait at spring. Okay?"

He was relieved that she didn't expect him to push the chair uphill and down to the far pasture, but — to wait alone with the old man? His heart began to pound faster. He licked his lips. "Okay," he said. "Sure."

Jupe looked at the girl and then at the chair, as though torn. When he realized that she was going and they were staying, he gave a yelp of delight and raced after her.

Now they were truly alone. Park turned the chair so the old man could see the moon, and set the brake. He started to sit down on the grass. It was damp, so he sat on his haunches Thanh-style a few feet from the chair. The afghan had come loose in the trip down the hill. He went over and squatted in front of the chair and began to tuck it close around the old pajamaed legs.

"Haaaa." There was nowhere to run. His heart had stopped, but Park made himself look up into the old face. Even in the shadows, he thought he could see tears. "Haaaa."

"What's the matter?" Park willed the words out of his mouth. "Does something hurt?"

The clawlike left hand came out from under the afghan and reached toward him. Park held himself tightly so as not to flinch, not to retreat. The back of the hand touched Park's cheek, then fell away. With an effort, the old man lifted the hand again. This time it went back and forth several times, cool and baby soft against Park's face. "Haaaa," he repeated. "Haaaa." The hand flopped heavily from Park's cheek to his own chest.

"Yes," said Park, suddenly understanding. "Park. You mean Park. I'm Park, and you're Park. That's what you mean, right?"

His grandfather turned his twisted head slightly, as if to nod, then repeated the stroke of Park's cheek and the touch of his own breast with gentle *haaaa*'s each time.

"Yes, we're both Park." Park could understand him! He was, if not making conversation, at least making contact with his grandfather. He wanted to grab the old hands or hug the old body. Suddenly the withered arm was flung out toward the sky.

"HAAAAAA!" the old man sobbed out. "HAAA-AAAA!" The arm fell lifeless to the side of the chair. There was no question now about the tears.

"What is it?" Park was crying too. "What is it? Do you miss him? Is that it?" But the pain in the eyes said more than grief.

"Don't cry, please don't cry." Park hugged the old knees. The sobbing did not lessen.

"What is it?" He stood up and took the wasted face between his hands and held it. His grandfather's tears wet his fingers. The tears were running down his own cheeks, too, catching in his glasses. He let them run. "What's the matter? Please tell me," he begged. And now, looking into the eyes, he saw his mother's eyes and his own eyes, as in a mirror. So that was it. "You think you killed him," Park said softly. "You think it's your fault."

Between his fingers, he could feel his grandfather's head move forward and back. He was nodding yes.

Park let the face go and put his arms around his grandfather's shoulders and held him tight while they both cried like lost three-year-olds returned at last to their mothers' arms.

"Gone!" Thanh was yelling as she ran down the

road, waving his bloodstained T-shirt above her head. "Gone!"

"Gone?" Not their crow. Not dead. Not now. "What happened?"

"Okay!" she cried. "Okay. Fly free!"

She threw him the T-shirt and ran past them into the springhouse. When she came out, it was slowly, carrying in both hands the coconut shell, filled to overflowing with cool, sweet water. "Now," she ordered. "Now. All drink."

Then they took the Holy Grail in their hands and drew away the cloth and drank of the Holy Wine. And it seemed to all who saw them that their faces shone with a light that was not of this world. And they were as one in the company of the Grail.

Bibliography

When we were planning this series of talks it occurred to us that we would like to know what books
these six writers of children's books remember with
particular affection from their own childhood or, as
adults, have found helpful or influential in their life
and work. This is their answer to our request for an
informal bibliography.

JEAN FRITZ

Rather than list specific sources for my books, I'd like
to name a few of the books that have sustained me.
They have earned a permanent place on my shelves.

BOOKS ABOUT BIOGRAPHY AND AUTOBIOGRAPHY

Since I know no biographers or autobiographers who are likely to drop in for shop talk over a morning cup of coffee, I have found companions and inspiration in books.

Marc Pachter, ed., *Telling Lives: The Biographer's Art* (New Republic Books, 1979). Seven well-known biographers talk about their craft. In my copy the sections by Marc Pachter and Leon Edel are the most heavily underlined.

Eric Homberger and John Charmley, eds., *The Troubled Face of Biography* (St. Martin's Press, 1988). Another collection. Here my favorite selections are by Robert Skidelsky and Michael Holroyd.

James Olney, *Autobiography: Essays Theoretical and Critical* (Princeton University Press, 1980). Although I don't plan to venture again into autobiography, this book contains so many starred passages, marginal notes and turned-down pages that it's bound to be a lifelong friend.

COMMENTARIES ON THE HUMAN CONDITION

Surely every biographer, every historian, perhaps every writer, is ultimately inquiring into the nature of the human condition.

Barbara Tuchman, *The March of Folly* (Knopf, 1984). An overview of history, highlighting those instances, from the Trojan War to the Vietnam War, when governments have deliberately pursued policies contrary to their interest, in spite of opposition, in spite of the fact that alternatives were available.

Milton Klonsky, *The Fabulous Ego: Absolute Power in History* (New York Times Books, 1974). Eighteenth-century readers who studied history as a succession of tyrants and were suspicious of power would have loved having this collection of power-mad despots within the covers of one book. I do.

Isaiah Berlin, *The Hedgehog and the Fox* (Simon & Schuster, 1953). Berlin draws on an old Greek saying that divides people into two categories: hedgehogs and foxes.

Alan Arkin, *The Lemming Condition* (Harper & Row, 1976). A hilarious but profound children's story in which a lemming refuses to do the lemming "thing."

OTHER CULTURES, OTHER PEOPLE, OTHER TIMES

It is imperative for me to take a vacation from twentieth-century America and look at life through other eyes. Indeed, most of my writing has been a series of such excursions.

Peter Gay, *The Enlightenment: An Interpretation* (Vintage, 1968). Many scholars have made me feel at home in the eighteenth century, but more than anyone else Peter Gay has helped me acquire the intellectual outlook I needed.

Jamake Highwater, *The Primal Mind: Vision and Reality in Indian America* (Harper & Row, 1981). Especially helpful as I was working on *The Double Life of Pocahontas*, but in any case a book I wouldn't want to miss.

Jonathan Spence, *The Gate of Heavenly Peace: The Chinese and Their Revolution 1895–1980* (Viking, 1981). All of Spence's books, marvels of detailed research and literary style, have been invaluable in my study of China.

John Hersey, *The Call* (Knopf, 1985). Since John Hersey and I were contemporaries in China and our fathers were colleagues, I took special joy in this fine, realistic novel.

Mark Salzman, *Iron and Silk* (Random House, 1986). An entertaining account of the author's two years in China, filled with anecdotes that in a remarkable way illustrate various facets of the Chinese personality.

CHILDHOOD

It is important for me to keep in contact not only with the child in me but with childhood itself.

C. S. Lewis, *Surprised by Joy: The Shape of My Early Life* (Harcourt Brace, 1955). A wonderful autobiography of a childhood in which the author feels free to come and go as an adult with his adult observations.

Antoine de Saint-Exupéry, *The Little Prince* (Harcourt Brace, 1943). Writers and children both can appreciate the frustration of the Little Prince when his drawing of a boa constrictor digesting an elephant is mistaken for a hat.

Florence Parry Heide, *The Shrinking of Treehorn* (Holiday House, 1971). A highly amusing read-aloud story for all ages that illustrates the difficulties of being a child in a world of grown-ups, recognizable but so dense that they seem almost to belong to another species.

MAURICE SENDAK

When we asked Maurice Sendak for a bibliography of the works that have influenced and inspired him, he directed us to his book Caldecott & Co.: Notes on Books and Pictures (*Farrar, Straus & Giroux, 1988*), *a spirited collection of thirty-two essays, talks and interviews in which he pays affectionate homage to a wide variety of writers and illustrators of books for children. We selected the following passages:*

From the first, my great and abiding love was William Blake, my teacher in all things. And from two other Englishmen, Thomas Rowlandson and George Cruikshank, I borrowed techniques and tried to forge them into a personal language. The Frenchman Boutet de Monvel refined my eye and quickened my heart and ambition. The Germans Wilhelm Busch and Heinrich Hoffmann provided me with the basis of a style and hinted at a kind of content that developed much later in my own work. When I was sixteen I first saw the edition of *Pinocchio* illustrated by Attilio Mussino, and I know that was a turning point. My eyes were

[180

opened by the offhand virtuosity of the man, the ease with which he commanded a variety of styles, controlling them all, blending them and still managing to keep them subservient to the tale. He taught me at one and the same time respect for finish and style as well as a certain disregard for these qualities. Style counts, I now saw, only insofar as it conveys the inner meaning of the text being illustrated.

Early in 1878, Randolph Caldecott began his illustration for some of the better-known [Mother Goose] rhymes, and no artist since has matched his accomplishments. Caldecott breathed life into the picture book. . . . As in a song, where every shade and nuance of the poem is heightened and given greater meaning by the music, so Caldecott's pictures illuminate the rhymes. This is the *real* Mother Goose — marvelously imagined improvisations that playfully and rhythmically bounce off and around the verse without ever incongruously straying. If any name deserves to be permanently joined with that of Mother Goose, it is that of Randolph Caldecott. His picture books should be among the first given to every child.

Hans Christian Andersen is infinitely more than a teller of sentimental tales; he is a poet. Through the

medium of the fairy tale, he found his original voice.
. . . Andersen was that rare anomaly, wise man and
innocent child; he shared with children an uncanny
poetic power, the power of breathing life into mere
dust. It is the intense life — honest, ingratiating — in
Andersen's tales that makes them unique.

George MacDonald was a novelist, poet, mythmaker,
allegorist, critic, essayist, and, in everything, a
preacher. One of the towering and mystifying figures
of Victorian literature, he wrote well over fifty
books, of which only two, *At the Back of the North
Wind* and *The Princess and the Goblin*, are still
widely read. His main forte was fantasy. . . . For
admirers of MacDonald, such as myself, his work has
something of the effect of a hallucinatory drug. Fin-
ishing one of his stories is often like waking from a
dream — one's own dream. The best of them stimulate
long-forgotten images and feelings — the "something
profound" that borders frustratingly close to memory
without quite ever reaching it.

Beatrix Potter's *Peter Rabbit* transcends all arbitrary
qualities. It is obviously no more a fact book about the
habits of rabbits than it is a purely fantastical tale. It
demonstrates that fantasy cannot be completely di-

vorced from what is real; that fantasy heightens and contributes new insights into that reality. . . . Altogether the book possesses, on no matter how miniature a scale, an overwhelming sense of life, and isn't that the ultimate value of any work of art? This standard should be applied to every book for the young, and no book can claim the distinction of art without it. *Peter Rabbit*, for all its gentle tininess, loudly proclaims that no story is worth the writing, no picture worth the making, if it is not a work of imagination.

Winsor McCay, the creator of [the comic strip] *Little Nemo in Slumberland*, has begun to receive the recognition he deserves. *Little Nemo* is an elaborate and audacious fantasy that suffers only slightly from the cramped space imposed by its form. It is, in effect, a giant children's book, though no more limited to children than *Alice in Wonderland* or the Grimm tales. McCay and I serve the same master, our child selves. We both draw not on the literal memory of childhood but on the emotional memory of its stress and urgency. And neither of us forgot our childhood dreams. *Little Nemo* is a catalogue of nightmares, a profusion of extreme fantasy images rendered with such explicit definition that the dream is captured in all its surrealistic exactitude. There are many details that I suspect only children see, and those few adults who still look with a child's intelligent curiosity.

Maxfield Parrish's first illustrated book, L. Frank Baum's *Mother Goose in Prose* (1897), already had the extraordinary Parrish qualities. Overflowing with good humor and imagination, these fine drawings in line and stipple offer elegantly patterned shapes and shrewdly composed blank areas. Parrish knew well the value of white space. His Baum pictures reveal a completely original vision that adds an otherworldly dimension to the book.

I discovered *Peacock Pie* when I jostled a shelf at the Argosy Book Shop in 1958. The book fell on my head. No one had prepared me for Lovat Fraser, and I'm grateful for that. I had the profound pleasure of finding him by myself, as well as the good sense to be influenced by his work and to collect thereafter everything by him I could lay my hands on. . . . His work embodies a point of view that is worth noting and incorporating into one's creative psyche. He was free of aesthetic snobbery. With the same care and integrity, with relish and joy that are altogether beguiling, he embellished, decorated and designed everything from charming ephemera to his glorious stage

[184

productions. No form was beneath him. His influence on my own work — my attitude toward my work — has been considerable.

Jean de Brunhoff's [*Babar*] books have a freedom and charm, a freshness of vision, that captivates and takes the breath away. Like a virtuoso poetic form, the interplay between few words and many pictures commonly called the picture book makes aesthetic demands that few have mastered. The best examples should rightfully take their place with comparable sophisticated "grownup" works of art. Jean de Brunhoff was a master of this form. Between 1931 and 1937 he completed a body of work that forever changed the face of the illustrated book.

The golden age of Mickey Mouse for me is that of the middle thirties. A gratifying shape, fashioned primarily to facilitate the needs of the animator, he exuded a sense of physical satisfaction and pleasure — a piece of art that powerfully affected and stimulated the imagination. . . . The Mickey who exerted influence on me as an artist is the Mickey of that early time — my early time. I only once broke cover and fused a very particular character [of mine] with the famous Mouse. That is the Mickey who is the hero of my picture book *In the Night Kitchen*. It seemed natural and honest to reach out openly to that early best friend while eagerly exploring a very private, favorite childhood fantasy. *In the Night Kitchen* is a kind of homage to old times and places — to Laurel and Hardy comedies and *King Kong*, as well as to the art of Disney, comic books in general, and the turn-of-the-century funny-papers fantasist Winsor McCay in particular.

JILL KREMENTZ

Any bibliography of mine has to start with Nancy Drew and Cherry Ames, Student Nurse: every title in both series of books. They seemed to be (even though they weren't) books about real women doing real things. It was the closest thing to nonfiction I could find at that age.

Here are some other books that have shaped the way I look at the world:

Henri Cartier-Bresson, *The Decisive Moment* (Simon & Schuster, 1952). When I began as a photographer, that book was my bible. I particularly like this sentence: "To me, photography is the simultaneous recognition, in a fraction of a second, of the significance of the event as well as of a precise organization of forms which give that event its proper expression."

Gordon Parks, *Flavio* (W. W. Norton, 1978). As a young photojournalist I was profoundly moved by all of his work, especially *Flavio*, a photo essay that first appeared in *Life*, and *A Choice of Weapons* (Harper & Row, 1965), a memoir. People are always asking photographers what kind of equipment they use. Gordon Parks said that when you photograph with your heart it doesn't matter what kind of equipment you use.

Dorothea Lange: A Photographer's Life by Milton Meltzer (Farrar, Straus & Giroux, 1978). A good biography of one of my idols. Also, *Dorothea Lange Looks at the American Country Woman* (Amon Carter Museum, Fort Worth, and Ward Ritchie Press, Los Angeles, 1967). Wonderful, strong photographs.

Portrait of Myself by Margaret Bourke-White (Simon & Schuster, 1963). Also, *You Have Seen Their Faces* by Erskine Caldwell and Margaret Bourke-White (Modern Age Books, 1937). When I first started out, there were only two women photographers I had heard of — Lange and Bourke-White. They were, of course, my great heroes, not only because they were women but because I wanted to be a photojournalist.

I greatly admire Walker Evans's work, especially his collaboration with James Agee, *Let Us Now Praise Famous Men* (Houghton Mifflin, 1941). It was the book that most inspired and influenced me when I did my own book about the South, *Sweet Pea*.

Lewis W. Hine and the American Social Conscience by Judith Mara Gutman (Walker & Company, 1967). The photographer Lewis Hine is another major hero, and this is the best book about him that I know.

Archibald MacLeish, *Land of the Free* (Harcourt Brace, 1938). A poem written to illustrate photographs taken during the Depression for the Resettlement Administration, which later became the Farm Security Administration.

Night Comes to the Cumberland: A Biography of a Depressed Area by Harry M. Caudill (Atlantic Monthly Press, 1963).

Robert Coles, *Farewell to the South* and *Children of Crisis, I: A Study of Courage and Fear* (Atlantic Monthly Press, 1972 and 1967). Coles is another of my heroes.

Four oral histories:

Estaban Montejo, *The Autobiography of a Runaway Slave* (Bodley Head, 1968).

Studs Terkel, *American Dreams: Lost and Found* (Pantheon, 1980).

Harlan Miners Speak: Report on Terrorism in the Kentucky Mine Fields, prepared by members of the National Committee for the Defense of Political Prisoners (Da Capo Press, 1970).

Oscar Lewis, *Children of Sanchez: The Autobiography of a Mexican Family* (Random House, 1961). Besides being an oral historian, Lewis is one of two anthropologists who have been important models for me because of their patient field work and their careful examination of everyday life. The other is Margaret Mead. Her books, such as *Growing Up in New Guinea* (William Morrow, 1930), are models of clear observation.

The two writers I most like to read now are E. B. White — especially two collections of essays, *The Second Tree from the Corner* and *The Points of My Compass* (Harper & Row, 1953 and 1962) — and Eudora Welty, above all for their language. I have two Welty favorites: *The Optimist's Daughter* (Random House, 1972), a novel, and *One Time, One*

Place: Mississippi in the Depression, A Snapshot Album* (Random House, 1971). I love snapshots, and Welty brings the same eye for detail and the same compassion and sense of caring to these snapshots that she does to her writing.

Anne Morrow Lindbergh, *The Flower and the Nettle: Diaries and Letters, 1936–1939* (Harcourt Brace, 1976). I like reading about women who were professional and who did what they did very well.

Alice Duer Miller, *The White Cliffs* (Coward Mc-Cann, 1940). When I was young my mother used to recite this wartime poem about the white cliffs of Dover aloud to me by heart, and it gave me a strong sense of cadence and of the rhythm of words, which I still try to observe, especially because parents often read my books aloud to their children.

Phyllis McGinley, *Love Letters* (Random House, 1954). It was because of one poem in this volume that I wrote *A Very Young Dancer*. The poem is "Portrait of Girl with Comic Book," and it begins, "Thirteen's no age at all." I had met a girl named Amy Robbins, whom I wanted to photograph to illustrate the poem. She happened to mention that she was studying ballet, and that's how it started — not just one book but the four other "Very Young" books that followed it.

Life Photographers: Their Careers and Favorite Pictures (Doubleday, 1957). This book was given to me on my first day as a *New York Herald Tribune* photographer. It was because *Life* was no longer around that I wrote *A Very Young Dancer* as a book and became a writer of books. Otherwise I'd still be pounding on their door asking them to do a six-page photo essay on a little girl who wants to be in the ballet.

Richard Meryman, *Hope: A Loss Survived* (Little, Brown, 1980). I love this book. It's Meryman's story of the death of his wife, Hope. It was a big help when I did *How It Feels When a Parent Dies.*

On a personal note, of course, I love my husband Kurt Vonnegut's books. My favorites (for what it's worth) are his two nonfiction collections, *Palm Sunday* and *Wampeters, Foma & Granfalloons* (Delacorte, 1981 and 1974).

JACK PRELUTSKY

*This bibliography is so
much more than merely biblio.*

It lists assorted background stuff,
thirty items — that's enough!

ABBOTT AND COSTELLO

"Who's on first?" (The answer's "Who!")
I miss you, Bud. I miss you, Lou.

WOODY ALLEN

His eye is keen, his humor's wry,
and he's from Brooklyn. So am I.

THE AMERICAN MUSEUM OF
NATURAL HISTORY

In here I gained a sense of awe
from whales and dinosaurs I saw.

THE BRONX ZOO

Polar bears and African plains
so near the elevated trains!

SID CAESAR

Oh how I admire
your clever satire.

We have the same birthday —
perhaps it's a mirthday.

LEWIS CARROLL

Turtle Soup and Hunt the Snark
Jabberwocky . . . what a lark.
You made me laugh, and I was glad
you thought to make your Hatter mad.

CARTOONS AND COMIC STRIPS

How wonderful the characters,
how strange the situations,
odder than most folks I know,
including my relations.

BILL COSBY

I love his humor,
he's a pro,
and so I borrow
from his show.

FOLK MUSIC

English, Irish, Scottish ballads,
I adored you more than salads,

and that was in my salad days,
before I'd ever tried soufflés.

GILBERT AND SULLIVAN

*There's nothing the matter
with G & S patter.*

RUBE GOLDBERG

*His marvelous machines
helped teach me ways and means.*

MILT GROSS

*I tink I luff him motch.
He het a luffly totch.*

THE GUINNESS BOOK OF WORLD RECORDS

*A treasury of matchless loot
to feed my trivial pursuit.*

O. HENRY

*He showed me the ironic twist,
and so I put him on my list.*

JOHNSON SMITH CATALOGUE

Holy mackerel! Squirting nickels,
plastic poop and rubber pickles!

LAUREL AND HARDY

Such folly, Stan and Ollie!
By golly, you were jolly!

EDWARD LEAR

Had the Owl and the Pussycat never left home
Prelutsky might never have penciled a pome.

GROUCHO MARX

What élan! What panache!
What a stunning mustache!

H. L. MENCKEN

He taught me The American Language,
now when I write I feel no anguage.

MOTHER GOOSE

The first to show me poetry,
as good a goose as a goose can be.

OGDEN NASH

Only he would have written about the cobra: "This
*   creature*
fills its mouth with venom, and walks upon its
*   duodenum."*
Perhaps he's my poetic pop,
I could go on, but I think I'll stop.

S. J. PERELMAN

A literary comic voice,
everything he wrote was choice.

EDGAR ALLAN POE

Poems of dread and tales of gore,
I'll forget him nevermore.

SCIENCE FICTION

Asimov, Isaac, and Bradbury, Ray,
led me through the Milky Way,

a fellow named Heinlein, another named Clarke
took me to galaxies out in the dark.

PETER SELLERS

I'm tickled by Clouseau, and Sellers
portrayed other wacky fellers.
His natal day? September 8,
just the same as my birth date.

ERNEST THOMPSON SETON

His tales of creatures in the wild
absorbed me when I was a child.
In his genre E. T. Seton
positively can't be beaten.

H. ALLEN SMITH

He wrote of jokers practical,
and never was didactical.

ROBERT LOUIS STEVENSON

I read his poems when I was wee
in Woman's Day *at the A & P.*

SUNDAY TIMES CROSSWORD PUZZLES

A splendid writing warmup,
they helped me keep my form up.

CHARLES WEISS

The funniest man in my family,
his silly stories tickled me,
my favorite uncle when I was a kid,
I wear suspenders because he did.

ROSEMARY WELLS

Fiction: These books I read for style. That's the same thing as going into a museum and staring at certain paintings or drawings before you begin to draw. It's like playing tennis with a backboard after watching Martina Navratilova play for an hour. What you see or hear gets into the brain somehow, and what comes out is not imitation but tempered prose. This is my "desert island" list of books.

Jack Finney, *Time and Again.* This is the best fantasy I've ever read for adults. It's also wonderful history, and the sheer inventiveness of it makes it a book to be rerelished every seven or eight years.

For pure beautiful writing, magnificent use of English and everything you might want to know about the human condition:

Evan Connell's *Mrs. Bridge*. I reread *Mrs. Bridge* before I write seriously. Close is Bruce Chatwin's *On the Black Hill* and Joyce Carol Oates's *them*. Also, the collected short stories of John Cheever and Elizabeth Bowen. Anything by the big Southern trio: Flannery O'Connor, Eudora Welty and Carson McCullers. Reading these women's books is like listening to Handel.

Nonfiction: Almost all I read in nonfiction is history. This has to include Barbara Tuchman's *The Proud Tower* and *The Zimmerman Telegram*, and William Manchester's Churchill books, like *The Last Lion*, which are super biography. Also, Fitzroy Maclean's *Eastern Approaches*, a wonderful adventure story of an English diplomat between the wars and during World War II as a partisan with Tito. In addition, Beryl Markham's *West with the Night*. Evan Connell again, *The White Lantern* and *A Long Desire*, two books about discovery that I reread frequently because of Connell's mastery of the language. These are books I learn to write from; there is always more to learn by rereading. Mary McCarthy's *Memories of a Catholic Girlhood* is excellent autobiography.

Mystery: I'm a mystery writer and I enjoy good thrillers. My all-time best mystery is Josephine Tey's *Miss Pym Disposes.* Anyone wanting to try this genre needs to think about the structure of this story; it's halfway done before you know it is a mystery. There is no policeman, so you don't know what will happen. Best of all, the clues are all hidden in character, and the resolution of the story is heartbreaking, obvious once it's read, and brilliant. So many mysteries, particularly Agatha Christie's, are artificial and awkward. This is a work of art.

In addition, the complete works of John le Carré and Dick Francis. One of the regrets of my life is that I have now read them all and must wait patiently for more fixes.

In children's books, the three writers I like most are Robert Lawson, William Steig and Tomi Ungerer. Else Minarik cannot be ignored, nor Hugh Lofting.

Steig has the most to teach picture-book writers. His books are written with gentle humor, excellent characters and great emotion. My favorites are *Amos and Boris, Sylvester, The Magic Bone* and *Dr. DeSoto.*

Ungerer is just as funny and warm in *The Beast of M. Racine* and *The Hat.*

Minarik's Little Bear series (illustrated by Maurice Sendak) should be read to every aspiring children's book writer because the books are timeless, childlike and funny without any gimmicks.

Robert Lawson's *Mr. Revere and I, The Fabulous Flight, Captain Kidd's Cat, I Discover Columbus* and *Ben and Me* introduced me to my lifelong love of history. As a child I read them each a hundred times. Lawson is a little dated, but so well educated. He has a great ear and a heart of gold. He stands up to time.

One more book that I use to teach with in writers' workshops is Robert Kraus's *Whose Mouse Are You?* It has emotional content, lots of action, a perfect plot, sympathetic characters and a surprise ending, and it's only sixteen lines long!

Some odds and ends: *The Dead* by James Joyce, *Sophie's Choice* by William Styron, *The Snow Goose* by Paul Gallico, and three movies: *The Lady Vanishes, The Lavender Hill Mob* and *Stairway to Heaven.*

KATHERINE PATERSON

BOOKS THAT HAVE SHAPED ME

Books read in childhood and youth that I still recommend:

The Bible, King James Version. I guess I belong to the last generation raised on the KJ. I still use the copy I was awarded at age eight when I recited the answers to the Westminster Shorter Catechism to my aunt Katherine Womeldorf, who was the champion catechism teacher of Rockbridge County, Virginia. I have used many translations since, including Greek and Japanese, but for a writer nothing beats the KJ for music and majesty.

I was also raised on a variety of hymn books, as we sang hymns a lot when I was young. I often think that it has been the music of the Christian faith that has kept me in the fold during those periods when intellect rebels and feelings die. I can't sing Bach's "Jesus, Priceless Treasure," Mozart's "Ave Verum," Brahms's "How Lovely Are Thy Dwellings" or Randall Thompson's "Alleluia" and remain agnostic.

A. A. Milne — we had them all in Hwaian. I can

recite several poems verbatim (well, almost verbatim), and I still think "Eeyore Has a Birthday and Gets Two Presents" (from *Winnie-the-Pooh*) is one of the great stories of all time for combining hilarity with poignancy.

Beatrix Potter's *Tale of Peter Rabbit*, plus anything else this terrific lady wrote and illustrated.

Kenneth Grahame's *Wind in the Willows*, which gave us Toad to make us laugh and The Piper at the Gates of Dawn to make us wonder.

Frances Hodgson Burnett's *Secret Garden*. I really don't know any writers of my generation who weren't deeply affected by this book. Despite its flaws, it is magic.

Kate Seredy, *The Good Master* et al. Seredy was a marvelous author-illustrator who somehow has been forgotten. I loved her books, but it took me forty years to realize that *The Singing Tree* was a powerful antiwar novel.

Marjorie Kinnan Rawlings, *The Yearling*. If you think this book didn't influence me, you haven't read my books.

Charles Dickens, *A Tale of Two Cities*. It tore my romantic young soul to shreds. I still think it's his best ending.

Alan Paton, *Cry, the Beloved Country*. It made me

face the dark side of myself as perhaps no other book has ever done.

Leo Tolstoy's *War and Peace,* first read when I was twenty-one, is still the best novel I've ever read, in scope and depth.

Sigrid Undset, *The Master of Hestviken* — up there with the masters.

Jane Austen: *Emma* is my favorite, but I still reread everything the woman wrote and hope to become a better writer thereby.

Theologians to whom I'm indebted:

C. S. Lewis: outside the Bible, my first theological reading. His *Mere Christianity* was a light in my adolescent darkness.

Dietrich Bonhoeffer: I wrote a master's thesis on his writing. For those who don't know him at all, I suggest *Letters and Papers from Prison.*

Karl Barth: Protestants who study theology can't miss him, but his last book, *The Humanity of God,* affected me more than the dogmatics, perhaps because it's short, simple and humble.

Kazoh Kitamori: a uniquely Japanese view of the Judeo-Christian faiths. His most famous work, *The Theology of the Pain of God,* has been translated into English (Atlanta, John Knox Press, 1965).

Bibliography

Other helpful thinkers:

Jacob Bronowski: *The Origins of Knowledge and Imagination*, *The Ascent of Man* and his essays in *The Norton Reader*. I can hardly get through a speech without quoting Bronowski. He can present any argument — scientific, intellectual, ethical — with clarity and grace.

Robert Coles: besides his volumes in the *Children of Crisis* series, *The Political Life of Children* and *The Moral Life of Children* should not be missed.

Freeman Dyson, *Weapons and Hope*. The most helpful and best-written book I know about the nuclear crisis.

Poets of my youth that I still read:

John Donne: also his sermons; but his sonnets, secular and sacred, are hard to beat.

George Herbert: as a rest from Donne's intellectual games, I still love him.

Gerard Manley Hopkins: the one poet I always have close at hand. No one moves me more.

William Shakespeare: no comment needed.

Emily Dickinson: back then I thought I understood her.

Novels of adulthood that I give away to friends:

Shusaki Endo, *Silence*. A novel that explores the

problem of the silence of God in the face of human suffering. I think it's the most profound spiritual novel I've ever read.

Anita Desai, *Clear Light of Day*. So beautifully written that I, who usually read for story (and this one's good), was forced to stop and reread pages to savor the language before I could go on.

Robertson Davies, *Leaven of Malice*. My favorite of this Canadian writer's pile of good books. It's screamingly funny on the surface, with a tough undercoat.

Mary Lee Settle, *Prisons*. This is not her National Book Award winner, but it's the one of Settle's books that I find myself giving to special friends. This is historical fiction at its best.

Anne Tyler, *Celestial Navigations*. Not one of her funniest nor one of her best sellers, but a book that makes you look at the peculiar people you know in a new way.

George Eliot, *Middlemarch*. I was required to dissect *Silas Marner* in the eighth grade, so it was forty years before I could force myself to take another look at Eliot. When I did I could hardly believe what I'd cheated myself of.

Writing about writing that I keep rereading:
Caroline Gordon, *How to Read a Novel*. I think

this wonderful book about reading and, of course, writing is out of print. Try to find it if you care about novels.

Flannery O'Connor, *Habit of Being* and *Mystery and Manners*. Reading O'Connor is like having a friend in the house who's a wonderful writer eager to share everything she knows.

Jill Paton Walsh, "The Lords of Time," an essay in *The Openhearted Audience* (Library of Congress, 1980). All the essays in this book on writing for children are worth reading, but Paton Walsh's is for me the best statement I know on what it means to write for the young.

A few of the many books I wish had my name on the cover and don't:
Ramona the Brave, Beverly Cleary
Homesick: My Own Story, Jean Fritz
Chance Child, Jill Paton Walsh
The Strange Affair of Adelaide Harris, Leon Garfield
Home Before Dark, Sue Ellen Bridgers
Is That You, Miss Blue?, M. E. Kerr
Tuck Everlasting, Natalie Babbitt
Charlotte's Web, E. B. White
Sarah, Plain and Tall, Patricia MacLachlan

Contributors

JEAN FRITZ was born in China of missionary parents and lived there until she was thirteen — a childhood that she describes in *Homesick*, which won the National Book Award and a Newbery Medal. A graduate of Wheaton College, she began her career by writing short stories that were published in *The New Yorker* and other magazines. She became interested in children's books, however, when her own two children reached reading age and she began working with young people at her local library. She is best known for her many lively biographies of historical figures, including Benedict Arnold, Christopher Columbus, Sam Houston, Stonewall Jackson, James Madison, Pocahontas, Paul Revere, Harriet Beecher

Stowe, and George Washington. For many years she conducted a writing workshop that has since resulted in more than one hundred published books. She lives in Dobbs Ferry, New York.

JILL KREMENTZ was born in New York and grew up in New Jersey. She studied anthropology with Margaret Mead and later became a staff photographer with the *New York Herald Tribune*, covering the civil rights movement — an interest that led to her first book, *Sweet Pea*, about a nine-year-old black girl growing up in Alabama in the 1960s. Her two dozen photo-essay books for children and young adults include the "Very Young" series, which depict various children's occupations (*A Very Young Dancer*, *A Very Young Gymnast*, etc.), and the "How It Feels" series, which deal with severe childhood traumas *(How It Feels When a Parent Dies*, *How It Feels When Parents Divorce*, *How It Feels to Be Adopted*, and *How It Feels to Fight for Your Life)*. She is also known for her photographs of authors, many of which are collected in her book *The Writer's Desk*. She lives in New York with her husband, Kurt Vonnegut, and their daughter, Lily.

KATHERINE PATERSON was born in China of American missionary parents and came to the United

States at the onset of World War II. She is a graduate of King College in Tennessee, of the Presbyterian School of Christian Higher Education in Virginia, and of Union Theological Seminary in New York. She studied and worked for four years in Japan. She is the author of twenty-five books that have been translated into twenty-two languages, including twelve novels for young people, two of which — *The Master Puppeteer* (1977) *and The Great Gilly Hopkins* (1979) — won the National Book Award. Two other books, *Bridge to Terabithia* (1978) and *Jacob Have I Loved* (1981), received the Newbery Medal, and in 1998 she received the Hans Christian Andersen Award for the body of her work. *Parzival,* her retelling of the epic poem, is her most recent book. She and her husband live in Barre, Vermont.

JACK PRELUTSKY was born in Brooklyn and grew up in the Bronx. After graduating from the High School of Music and Art he sporadically attended Hunter College, where he managed to flunk seven language classes, including English. His first book of poems, *A Gopher in the Garden,* was published in 1967, and he has since written more than thirty books of children's poetry, including *Nightmares, The Dragons Are Singing Tonight, The New Kid on the Block, A Pizza the Size of the Sun,* and *The Beauty of the Beast.*

He has compiled many anthologies, including *The Random House Book of Poetry for Children*. His latest book is a collaboration with Lane Smith and the late Ted Geisel (Dr. Seuss), which completes some of Geisel's unfinished notes, verses, and sketches, called *Hooray for Diffendoofer Day!* Prelutsky and his wife live on an island near Seattle.

MAURICE SENDAK, Brooklyn-born, first illustrated the books of other children's writers — Ruth Krauss's *A Hole Is to Dig* (1952), the Little Bear books by Else Holmelund Minarik, and stories by Isaac Bashevis Singer and Randall Jarrell. He became both writer and illustrator with *The Nutshell Library* (1962), followed by *Where the Wild Things Are* (1963), which won the Caldecott Medal; *Higglety Pigglety Pop!* (1967); *In the Night Kitchen* (1970); *Outside Over There* (1981); *Dear Mili* (1988), his interpretation of a story by Wilhelm Grimm; and *We Are All in the Dumps with Jack and Guy* (1993). For his body of work he has received both the Hans Christian Andersen Award — the first American illustrator so honored — and the Laura Ingalls Wilder Award of the American Library Association. In 1997 he received the National Medal of Arts from President Clinton. He has designed the sets and costumes for five operas and is cofounder of Night Kitchen, a children's theater company. He lives in Connecticut.

ROSEMARY WELLS, author of more than fifty books, was born in New York and grew up on the New Jersey shore. With the creation of the bunny Max and his bossy older sister, Ruby, she invented the toddler's indestructible "board book." Those small volumes, printed on heavy cardboard, feature Max in many of childhood's defining moments: *Max's First Word*, *Max's New Suit*, *Max's Christmas*, etc. For an older audience of four- to seven-year-olds her most popular picture books are *Noisy Nora*, *Benjamin and Tulip*, and *Timothy Goes to School*. For her "oldest young readers" she writes mysteries — notably, the Edgar Award–winning *When No One Was Looking*. In 1996 she illustrated Iona Opie's *My Very First Mother Goose*. Her campaign to promote reading aloud to young children, "The Most Important Twenty Minutes of Your Day," which brought her an invitation to the White House, has been adopted by several states. She lives just north of New York City.